A QUIVER OF GUID

C000062706

By the same autho

Holy Ghostbuster

Yesterday's People

Privies of North Wales

Privies of Wales

Operation Woolsack

Poble Ddoe

Yr Anhygoel

Extracts ...

The Spirit Guide:

"We face a German SS firing squad. I don't want to look but I had to turn to where my friends are. How do they face their death? Like me? Nervous? I turn my head. Next to me there is a priest. Where did he come from? He was not there before!

"His face is smiling, but not smiling. A sort of calm smile that isn't a smile but is. It cannot be explained. He is not looking at me but talking to me and only to me. He says: *'Put your chest out. Look ahead. I will be with you now and tomorrow. You are with me'.* Then he smiles; this is a real smile. I look ahead and heave my chest. I am drunk in my head not knowing what to think. Think about being shot or think about where the priest came from. I wish I had time to think about both things at the same time … *then the order came to halt the execution….*

Ziggy Bossowski, Polish Army Lieutenant WWII

The Poltergeist:

"It was during our third meeting with poltergeist Harold that it happened. Harold was being evasive about the date and manner of his death. He was refusing to tell us where he had been buried. Suddenly Elwyn Edwards said to him; "You haven't crossed have you Harold?" Harold shook his head in agreement. I could have kicked myself for not having thought of this before. It was so obvious. It had been staring at us in the face every time we had spoken to him. Harold Yates was an earth-bound ghost!"

Harold the Poltergeist

CONTENTS

<u>Trilogy</u>

'Quiver of Guides and Poltergeist' completes a trilogy of authored works centred on the Rev. J. Aelwyn Roberts's extraordinary career in dealings with the paranormal and in his beliefs in life after death.

For detail of how to order '*Holy Ghostbuster*' and '*Yesterday's People*' (Welsh translation: *Poble Ddoe*) which complement this book, please refer to the rear pages.

ACKNOWLEDGEMENTS

Elwyn Roberts

I feel sure that like myself, **Elwyn Roberts** will come to regard this book, "*A Quiver of Guides and Poltergeists*" as a sort of official ending to a lifetime of ghost-hunting, ghost be-friending and ghost counselling. There is no doubt we will both be tempted to don our topees and safari jackets from time to time for further, occasional, midnight expeditions. But for both of us, this book will mark the end of a fantastically interesting partnership. Other people have formed friendships based on football watching, bird-watching and train watching.

Ours is the strangest of them all.

Thank you, Elwyn, for everything we have been able to learn together about the paranormal and for the very happy hours we have spent together; often in some very uncomfortable situations.

It has been so well worth it. When our time comes to cross there will be no fear. It will, for both of us, be an experience even more exciting than any we have experienced in our sessions together.

Professor David Fontana

My good friend **David Fontana** has very kindly given me his permission to include in this book his full report, commissioned by the *Society for Psychical Research* on the alleged poltergeist activities of 'Pete' in Cardiff. The SPR is a highly intellectual organisation with a membership drawn from a myriad of disciplines. My friend David is its past president. I am deeply indebted to him for allowing me (*verbatim*) use of his well-researched paper. It allows me to demonstrate what level of care, caution and vigilance members of the Society employ in researching their subjects before allowing themselves to say that the disturbance or whatever has been reported, was caused by an entity from beyond the grave. They are the experts. They are the professionals.

Mark Roberts

For my last two books, '*Privies of Wales*' and '*Operation Woolsack*' and particularly for this, '*A Quiver of Guides and Poltergeists*' **Mark** has been a tower of strength. His cartoons and eye for good design have in the past invoked a great deal of interest. With his past newspaper experience and contacts he is also a fast researcher. His many talents have contributed greatly to the accuracy and content of this book.

I'm particularly grateful to Mark for introducing me in 1994 to the story of Ziggy Bossowski and for introducing me also those colleagues of his from within British airborne forces who validated the extraordinary story of Ziggy's spirit guide. No book on guides would be complete without it.

John and Anne Spencer

Those prolific writers of all-things ghostly who would so often quote extracts of my earlier books in their *'Encyclopaedia of Ghosts and Spirits'*. I am grateful for their reciprocal consents enabling me to mention their research in this book.

"Fleet Street"

That collective otherwise known as the national newspaper industry; so shy or timid to treat the science of 'ghostology' with anything more scant than the occasional Halloween readers' teaser - unless of course a TV soap, sport superstar or teenybopper celeb utters some profound comment on the matter.   My editorial friends in *Fleet Street* will therefore be astonished to find that so many of their own journalist colleagues have been pivotal to so many of the past Century's most astonishing accounts of spirit guides and poltergeists. Hannan Swaffer of the *Sunday People*, George Fallows of the *Daily Mirror*, Janet Grosse, the young journalist who died so early in life, Dr. John Le Fanu, medical correspondent for the *Sunday Telegraph*, Peter Liefhebber, the Dutch reporter; even my own son, Mark, an ex-Fleet Street tabloid 'hack' has contributed so positively.   Whether my gratitude is welcome or not, I thank *"Fleet Street"* for their great contribution.

Gareth Cowell

Thanks too to **Gareth Cowell** who, in laboriously proof-reading the drafts, generously allowed me to retain my not always grammatically correct style of writing.

My Printers

I also seem to have found for myself the most efficient and friendly of printers; **MFP Design & Print** of Manchester. To them, my thanks.

Book Council of Wales

What is printed also has to be carried around the country and offered on a weekly basis to shops, tourist centres and libraries. This humdrum chore is one that has been carried out for all my books by the **Books Council of Wales** to whom I am grateful.

And finally ...

The greatest debt, however, is owed to those very many thousands of readers spread around all corners of the world who embraced *"Holy Ghostbuster"* in any of its original or reprint forms and whose thirst for more inspired me to write *"Yesterday's People."* From that book grew another swell of reader interest leading to publication of this, the last in the trilogy ... and my final curtain call.

Thank you all.

Chapter One

I Am The Prologue

It has always annoyed me. Whenever or wherever I go to speak in public on the subject of ghosts and things pertaining to the paranormal that the chairman of the meeting, or the presenter of the radio or television programme, always feels obliged during his introduction to build up some kind of atmosphere of fear.

"And now," he will say, "I have to introduce to you our speaker for tonight. Hold fast to your seats all of you because I have a feeling that we are all going to hear things tonight that will make our hair stand on end. Something tells me that none of us is going to sleep very soundly in our beds tonight." Why ever not Mr Chairman?

The point he is trying to make is that I am going to speak about ghosts, and in his opinion ghosts are always beings, things, or whatever that create fear. If he had been able to tell the audience that I was about to speak about some of their grandparents there would have been no need to sound the warning bells. In fact, when I do speak to people about their ghosts I am, more often than not, speaking to them about their own ancestors; some from the same generation.

I entitled my earlier ghost-book *"Yesterday's People"* because, for me, ghosts are just that; yesterday's people. Ghosts are the ordinary men, women and children who used to live here on earth some many, many years ago. Others could have lived here so recently that we could have known them during their earth life. But they are now dead and living in a new world, or plane, or sphere or call it what you will. For some unknown reason some of them are able to return to their old earth haunts and are seen by the new tenants of the earth they used to inhabit. Nothing at all to fear. I can honestly say that I have never, in my life, been confronted by a violent or objectionable spirit.

I have talked to ghosts, I have listened to ghosts and even shared a few jokes with ghosts. But I have never had cause to be afraid of one. Many will say I can count myself lucky because there are, in spite of the honeyed words used at many funerals, many nasty, cruel, thuggish people who cross over to the other side every day. And I agree. But lucky or not I can still say that the majority of the spirits I have met, and they are legion, have been nice homely people. True I have met one or two odd bods from the spirit world, as I have in this world met quite a number of fruitcakes, but none that would make me feel afraid.

So when the meeting chairperson presents me as a sort of Frankenstein *cum* Bella Lugosi *cum* Boris Karloff, character all rolled into one, it does make me wonder what kind of talk he or she expects me to give.

As a matter of fact a good number of the ghosts whom I have met have been rather gormless and even uninteresting. They seem to waft about at odd hours carrying out peculiar tasks that only they find useful. When I spend an evening with earth friends I invariably come away having learnt something new. I often say of my old friend Gwenno Caffell that one only has to be in this lady's company for five minutes and you come away having learnt something absolutely fascinating. But I can't say this of my ghost friends. Many of them are utterly boring.

During a lifetime of associating with ghosts I have gleaned very little direct knowledge from them although I have to admit that I have probably picked up a few good habits and a few ideas from them. Many of us humans find it so difficult to terminate meetings; to take our leave graciously. There is nothing more annoying than the behaviour of a visitor who suddenly slaps his knees, stands up and says, "Well, that's it then folks, you'll have to excuse me – must be off!" and then stays another fifteen minutes humming and hawing, keeping the rest of the family on their feet because he has no idea how to take his leave.

Ghosts are not like that. They walk into a circle and take their place without any fuss. When they feel they have had enough they just slap their knee, stand up, and leave. Often when they fail to understand a question they will just walk away without a by your leave.

My children tell me that I am a bit like my ghosts in this respect. I visit their homes and when I think it is time to leave, they say I just get up and go. They also say that I sound abrupt and dismissive when I talk to them on the phone. They have never said whether or not they consider this trait in their father to be a good or bad one. I would think that if we, and especially company secretaries, could all cut out the telephone waffle of "*Long time no see, nice weather we are having,*" etc., 'phone bills would be cut at a stroke.

One of the most difficult things for a preacher who does not use a script, is to know when to draw his sermon to a tidy close; to find the right kind of ending. I don't know whether or not it is because of ghost influences, but I find myself these days after 13 or 15 minutes in the pulpit bringing my sermon to an abrupt end by simply saying, "That's it. Now we'll sing hymn 405'.

There is something too that ghosts have been trying to tell me about suicides. I have never been able to reconcile myself to the teaching that suicide is a sin that has to be cruelly purged away in the afterlife. I regard suicide as an illness; a sort of terminal depression. But the few ghost suicides I have met seem to say differently. They seem to remain desperately unhappy even in the life beyond.

I remember seeing the one who had taken up the womb position and he was crying. We found him in a sort of damp cleft in a rock. He told us that he was too ashamed to contact his parents and family in his new abode because he was so ashamed of what he had done. I'm still not too sure about this one. I hesitate to believe that suicide carries a punishment with it that extends even into life after death. It is more likely that the grief and the pain that causes a man to take his own life is so great that it takes a longer time to heal than any other. I have no doubt that in time it will wear off and the sad entrant into Paradise will take his place once more with his family and his friends. It just means that these poor souls in life were carrying a heavier pack of unhappiness in their lives than most of us. It just means that with such acute illness, convalescence takes a little bit longer. But it will heal. It always does heal

My name over the many years has become so linked with the paranormal and with ghosts that readers will find it difficult to believe that when I am invited to give an after-dinner talk I nearly always try and steer away from the subject of ghosts. They are really not my favourite topic. Certainly not for after dinner talks.

I sit at the end of the table with the chairperson and he gets up and says to his quietly burping guests: "Our speaker tonight is going to speak to us about "Old Welsh Customs." You can almost hear the groan of disappointment. I have never read a ghost book, I never look at ghostly films, and when any of my grandchildren - and I have many - delicately approach the subject of the paranormal by asking "Taid, have you ever seen a ghost?" I always pretend that I am scared of ghosts and that if I saw a ghost I would run a mile!

I have always regarded my entry into the spirit world as part of my work as a parson. I hesitate to describe it as my second vocation, although I have been able through my study to bring quite a lot of comfort to a great number of people - and I have letters from many different countries to prove it.

Over forty years ago the bishop appointed me as Director of Social Services for the Diocese of Bangor. The Social Work Office in any diocese is the one that tackles special problems. It exists so that busy parish priests can seek advice on how to tackle special and unusual problems that arise in the parish.

My office at the time was specially geared to help unmarried mothers. It was registered as an official Adoption Society and it also had throughout North Wales foster homes with couples who were prepared to look after babies until the little natural mothers could decide whether or not they would have to place them for adoption. It was a busy time. Roughly 500 babies were placed for adoption and their natural mothers kept a further 500 and more during this period when my wife and I carried out our work of Fostering and Adoption. Then the drug addicts and the alcoholics, like the poor, were also 'always with us'. But strangely one of the first problems to be hurled at me as the new director was a ghost problem. And a poltergeist problem at that.

It was a vicar's wife telling me that there was a couple seated in her Vicarage drawing room, determined not to leave until they had had a word with the vicar. She told me how they had come home from work to find their home ravaged, its furniture toppled over, carpets rolled, crockery smashed. The doors and windows were all locked, so this, they said, had to be the work of a ghost or a devil and they point-blank refused to go inside the house until the vicar arrived home to accompany them in. She then whispered into the phone "Bill is out visiting in the village. When he comes home he will be terrified; he's scared stiff of ghosts. Please can you do something quick."

From that day on I knew that I would have to swot up my ghosts if I was to make a go of my new job.

I have to admit that I have found dealing with ghosts rather boring. Given the choice of a good natter in a friend's house or sitting on a box in a haunted house waiting for 'himself' to make his appearance, I know which I would chose. On the other hand I have friends who envy me my job and covet my invitations to sit in ghost-ridden houses until all hours. So envious are they that they would willingly give a months pay to be able to come with me.

I have worked it out that it is not the ghosts, so much as the mystery which underlies their appearances, that intrigues me. I see them and I talk to them. The next day I find myself still asking if I did really see the form of a dead person or did I see a picture or ectoplasm or whatever. Then I always find myself asking if they are real people who have died; why it is that only the more dim-witted seem to appear to me - never the intelligent ones. When the Spiritualist Church was set up in the last century it had a great number of intellectual adherents – Bertram Russell, Morris Barbanell, Hannen Swaffer and hordes of others. Many of these promised they would make every effort to return to earth after death … but they never did.

And this is something which has puzzled me greatly. Prominent intellectual members of the Spiritualist Church anxious to cross back after death to witness the truth of their belief in life after death are unable to return. Bertrand Russell, if I remember correctly, almost boasted that he would come back - but never did. And yet others who were neither as intelligent nor involved during their life in spiritualist matters seem to come back in their thousands. The old undertaker from Bala who had lost all his children; the young husband who came back nightly to sit on the bottom of his wife's bed. These were ordinary people of this world. They couldn't be described as intelligent or clever, they had never shown any kind of interest in life after death and yet they just came back to earth as if it was the most natural thing in the world to do.

It's a puzzle.

I wonder? I wonder? I wonder? Is this perhaps because we on earth live in a domain where intelligence is king? A sphere where only cleverness is rewarded; clever scientists, clever writers of books and television soaps, people clever at kicking a football or singing a pop song. At least these are the people who in life live in large mansions, drive big cars, fly First Class when we, the not so clever are packed into Economy. These are the 'clever' people who seem to reap all the benefits and privileges of earth life.

Could it possibly be that in the other life, greatness is measured not by a man's intelligence, but by his humility? That in the other life it is the humble who are being asked for their autographs and not the clever, and that it is the humble who are given the privileges and not the talented?

I think particularly of Richard Wynne, the ghost who attended most our meetings in Bryntirion, North Wales. He was the undertaker who had lost six children before they had reached adolescence. His wife had blamed him for carrying the germs and diseases of the dead into their home. It was so humble the way he cried and accepted his fate. And the way he thanked us for our company. Humble Richard Wynne crossed without any effort at all.

There was the farmer husband who crossed over every night with the greatest of ease just to sit on the edge of his wife's bed to tell her how very sorry he was to have betrayed her and her children by committing suicide and to plead for her forgiveness. He wasn't clever; he didn't have a GCSE to his name. But he was very humble.

When the Blessed Lord came to choose His disciples and the leaders of his church, it was humble fishermen and tax collectors that he chose. He didn't have a single graduate amongst them; or a company director. Judas Iscariot was possibly the most intelligent of them all … and he was a failure.

I have a very high opinion of Spiritualists - the people who seem to deal professionally with the spirits of the departed and who weave their religious beliefs around the things that await us in the Afterlife. I have found them to be such nice people. Whether it is that nice people are attracted to this kind of belief or whether this kind of belief procreates nice people I will probably never know. Suffice to say that many of my best friends are Spiritualists.

When I strike up a conversation with a person in a train I find it impossible to discover whether or not my new companion is a Christian. We of the orthodox religions pride ourselves on not wearing our religion on our sleeves. But Spiritualists are not like that. There is something that is soft and warm about their beliefs. There is none of that dogmatic hardness of belief that is shared by the Anglican, and the Roman, and the Orthodox churches. I have a feeling that Spiritualists would be shocked if they knew members of all three of the mainstream Christian churches recite the Athanasian Creed together in their services and use the words:

"And we believe that they who have done good shall go into eternal life; and those who have done evil into everlasting fire. This is the Catholic Faith, which except a man believe faithfully, he cannot be saved."

The Spiritualists call the Afterlife '*Summerland*'.

There is no place in their beliefs for a nail-biting Day of Judgement. The newly dead, they say, gravitate to the kind of life and the kind of companions they enjoyed in their former lives. The person who has lived a foul, dishonest, and deceitful life on this earth, will at death soon locate or discover the hovels of others that had lived a similar foul, dishonest and deceitful life. He will abide with them because these are the kind of people he knows: their way of life is the only way he understands. The person who has lived a clean and honest life on earth will, however, gravitate towards those who also love a clean and honest life of culture. And all this is possible, the Spiritualists tell us, because Jesus said that, 'In His Father's House there are many mansions'.

The Summerland of these kind people is entirely different from the Paradise of the Anglicans, and the Purgatory of the Roman Catholics. Summerland knows nothing of Eternal Damnation and Everlasting Fire. If the foul-mouthed hooligan should ever begin to feel unhappy in his sin hovel he is always free to pack his bags and gravitate to another mansion. There is always hope for him.

The Spiritualists will never pray that those who have died be given Eternal Rest. Sleeping and resting is the very last thing one is encouraged to do in Summerland. They do concede that new spirits are allowed a short break, or a recuperative holiday, to get over the shock and the trauma of passing over. After this he is asked what kind of work he would like to do and will he need re-training for it. We say: "We believe in the resurrection of the dead." They say similar but with more conviction; "We *know* there is a resurrection of the dead." They know, they tell us, because many of the dead have returned to their members and have described to them the kind of life they lead in Summerland

I have met a good many of those who have returned from the *Afterlife* but I can't say that any of them have bothered to tell me anything about the way they lived. On the other hand it is equally true that I have never thought of telling them how life here on earth has changed for many of us OAP's since their time. That far from going to our beds without even locking our doors, as in the olden days, some of us are now too afraid to venture out to the chip-shop after dark.

Having said all this I now have to say that the Spiritualist religion could never satisfy my inner needs. Their teaching is far too narrow for me. They concentrate on just the one facet of the Christian Faith. Or, to be fair, one can say they 'specialise' in one facet of the Christian Faith only. I have come to think of the Anglican Church as my General Practitioner in matters of the soul. But I turn to the Specialist for my knowledge of life-after-death. My Specialist has taken away from me all fear of death. But I have news for all Anglican and Roman Catholic Bishops and for all non-conformists Moderators. I am not the only member of the church who uses the Spiritualist Church as a consultant in matters of life-after-death. When I very occasionally visit a midweek séance I meet a good number of 'church regulars', especially those who have suffered a recent bereavement. And the Spiritualist knowledge of healing is particularly good. I know because I have tried it.

My church has in recent years just started to re-kindle this Gift of Healing that was given to the Early Church and, sadly, lost. Up to now, however, I think I would still take my tennis elbow to the séance rather than the Anglican-healing Circle.

'*Prove all things; Hold fast to that which is good*.'

1 Thessalonians 5:21

Chapter Two

The Warm Up

Some say the business of seeing and talking to ghosts is rubbish, others say that it's sinful whilst again others are so fascinated with the idea that the dead can return to earth that they are prepared to spend even their housekeeping money buying the books that tell them all about it. I have a feeling it was a Professor Joad, a veteran television presenter on a programme called "Brain's Trust" a very long time ago who used to encourage his questioners and fellow panellists to define their terms before trying to give an answer to any problem.

I thought that a wonderful idea, so I "warm up" by including my own definition:-

> "A spirit, or ghost, is a human person whose body after a period of like on earth has died and has then put on a new spirit body. His heart has died, his body has died, and his brain has died and all these appurtenances he had in life are buried in the earth, or burned in fire. The only part of the human body that remains alive is the mind. The mind, or the ego, or the personality or the soul is the only part of the earth body, which doesn't survive. It is the one part that passes over to the afterlife…"

I have no idea how many lives, or existences, we have to pass through but my friends the spiritualists suggest it to be seven. I do know, however, that through all these different lives we take our original human earth mind with us. A good soldier never surrenders his sword except perhaps to his Field Marshal. A soul never hands over his mind except in eternity and then to the Creator who gave it to him in the first place.

Immediately after death – and probably while the doctor and the family are still in the sickroom or around the hospital bed – the dead person, having discarded his earth body, puts on his new spirit body. Both bodies look outwardly alike. This is why, when we see the ghost of Uncle William standing on the staircase in the middle of the night, we immediately recognise him as our loveable Uncle William. He appears to us very much as he did when he was alive and when he used to come and visit us at home. But although

Uncle William seems to appear to us in the same old body that we can identify with, we also realise that this cannot be the case. We were present at the churchyard when Uncle William's body and coffin were lowered into the grave. We also know that the body, which was lowered six-feet under or consumed by fire in the crematorium, was the physical earth body that we, the living, all employ to carry out those physical earthly tasks of ours. We kick a ball with it, we lift weights, mow the lawn with it, climb mountains with it and make love with it. Without the earth body, with its muscles and sinews, we are no longer able to perform the physical earth tasks we do while alive.

All the ghostology I know is self-taught. Even the name itself, "ghostology" is a home-made word; my home-made descriptive for something unquantifiable.

My job (and I have always regarded is as a *job*), has enabled me to meet a great variety of different ghosts. Some of them had been making nuisances of themselves to the new tenants of their erstwhile homes. People who pay high mortgages are reluctant to share their kitchens with spirit-squatters. The day after a visit to a haunted house, I write a little report of all that has happened.

But the whole thing has to make sense to me – and it has to be logical. Even spirits have to obey a reasonable code of behaviour. Human behaviour is governed by the human mind and thus human actions are predictable. Spirit behaviour is also governed by the human mind and so we have every right to expect spirit actions to be also predictable.

This is why when people tell me, as so very often happens, that they have a ghost in the house and that this ghost moves objects around in the house, I do become just a little bid dubious. I have been told so often by people: "I left my handbag on the table last night. When I came downstairs in the morning it wasn't there. I found it hanging on a peg in the hall."

I find this very difficult to believe. Even the moving of an object as light as a handbag from one place to another is an act that requires human muscles and sinews and nerves to direct both into action. Could he have moved it with his spirit body, someone will ask. But there is little or no evidence of this. The only evidence we have is the testimony given by rather absent-minded ladies who are willing to swear that they left the handbag on the table – when they hadn't.

Our earth body is specially designed to enable us to carry out earth tasks and our spirit body is equally designed to enable us to carry out spirit tasks. The spirit 'body' is far more complicated than the earth design. In motorcar language the spirit 'body' is the Mark II model compared with the Mark I of the earth version. Encased in this body, the spirit can walk though solid walls. He can travel at phenomenal speeds and can be present in several places at the same time. He can cope with living on a plane where time is in the Eternal Present – where past, present and future is all one.

I have found that the thing that confuses ghosts the most is coping with dates. Ask a spirit the question "when did you die?" or "when did you move to America?" and it becomes totally confused. Many will just walk away from such questioning. The reason possibly is that in the same way many of us today find it difficult to adapt to or answer questions about the old system of pounds, shillings and pence after getting used to the metric system, so spirits find it difficult remembering their old past, present or future days on earth after getting used to the eternal present of the Afterlife.

Some spirits (but not all) and again using their new bodies, are able to return for outings to the places favoured when they lived on earth. But although they can do all these clever things, I am convinced they can no longer clobber a person over the head with a hockey stick, nor move a handbag from the hall table onto a coat-peg on the wall – because these are exclusively human acts. No. I still maintain a spirit who moves things does not make sense. I say this in full knowledge that in further chapters I shall be describing how some 'ghosts' lift super-human weights, throw stones at targets and can talk. These ghosts are the exception to the role – to all rules. They are called poltergeists. If my lady with the missing handbag would ask me: "and what makes you think my ghost is not a poltergeist then Vicar?" I would say to her; "Madam, if you had a poltergeist in your house you would jolly well know about it!"

Then there is the other hard-to-believe ghost. This one is the 'standing at the foot of the bed' type. The story goes roughly as follows: "I was laying in bed not able to sleep, worrying about my operation the next day. I looked up and there was my mother standing at the foot of my bed. She was as clear to me as you are now. She didn't say anything. She just smiled. I was no longer afraid, and I knew I'd be all right the next day.

I have a feeling that most of these tales describe an 'apparition' rather than a ghost.

Throughout our lives, our super computer brain has been taking in billions of photographs or everything we have seen. All these have been carefully filed in the memory for future use. I have only to close my eyes, even in broad daylight, and I can see visualise how my mother looked with her long hair tied in a bun. I can also see how she looked the first time I saw her and after she had had her hair bobbed in the post Great War style. I can even remember her expression of disappointment when I cried after seeing her with her hair cut short. I must possess thousands of images of my mother; thousands more of my father, my grandparents, children, friends, colleagues … all filed away over 84 years of life.

I have a feeling, therefore, that it could have been one of these memory photographs of her mother that the operation lady saw standing at the foot of the bed. On the other hand, who am I to say?

The other interesting thing about this type of story is the way the old mother is said to be smiling at her daughter. Smiling is just about as far as solemn ghosts are allowed to go. I don't think I have ever heard of a ghost enjoying a good belly laugh. You never hear anyone telling the tale of a person lying in bed and saying; "I was just dozing off, sort of half-asleep, wondering about tomorrow, and I looked up in a kind of stupor and there was my father standing at the foot of the bed and he was killing himself laughing. He said to me: '*John, I heard this corker of a story today ...*' and between splutters of laughter went on to tell me the funniest joke I have every heard in my life. We were killing ourselves laughing the two of us. When I woke in the morning, try as I could, I just couldn't remember what the joke was about but my ribs were still aching with laughing."

That account, someone will say, just has to be a made-up story because ghosts don't laugh. Don't they just!

I am absolutely convinced that there is a lot of laughing and tomfoolery and leg-pulling going on in the other life. And I have proof of it!

Elwyn Roberts and I had been called to a house on a massive council estate. Before we had had time to take off our coats there was a ghost impatient to talk to us. We had never before met a more garrulous ghost. She told us that she was a trainee nurse who used to work in a nearby hospital. She had become pregnant, hadn't the nerve to tell her parents, so she had committed suicide on the very sport where we were standing. This, she told us, happened in 1934. She repeated the 1934 – the year she had died.

I have never seen a ghost like this one. No sooner had the question been asked than it was answered. The replies were careful and deliberate and emphasised. It was as if the young nurse had known that the old parson taking notes of her conversation wanted to make sure that it was an accurate report. She had committed suicide near a stream in the field where we were standing. There was a farm about 50 yards away; its name was Bryn Llwyd Isaf. Just in order to have more facts that could be easily checked, I asked her where she had been buried. The answer was again deliberate. She had been buried, she said, in her hometown of Llanberis in North Wales. She had been laid to rest in the burial ground of Capel Coch – the Red Chapel. I was then given explicit instructions as to how to find her grave. What a co-operative ghost I thought.

"When you arrive at Capel Coch you will find it has a long flight of wide stone steps leading to its three front entrances. Walk up the stairs, and when you come up to the middle entrance look to your left. There in the far corner, to the left you will see my grave with a white stone on it," she said. I drove home that night with a scribble pad bulging with notes. I could hardly wait for the morning to check my information – her information. It seemed unreasonable that there could have been a stream, and a farmhouse, where this colossal housing estate now stood, as recently as 1934. But there it was on the old ordnance map and clearly shown. The name of the farm was Bryn Llwyd Isaf – the name that our little nurse had so clearly spelled out; and the stream was also marked. The river Adda. I was feverish with excitement. But when I went to consult the census list at the County archivist's office in Caernarfon, a blank was drawn. They had no knowledge of the farmer or his wife; the names our young lady had given us. But I persevered all day and the next until I came eventually to the final clue; the burial place at 'Capel Coch'.

Non-conformist chapels are usually named after towns and villages in the Holy Land such as Bethesda, Bethsaida, Carmel, Horeb and Jerusalem. Capel Coch, the Red Chapel, sounded a real misnomer. When I arrived in Llanberis I asked a lady if she knew if there was a Capel Coch anywhere in the village. "Yes," said the lady and she proceeded to give me instructions. "This road to your left," she pointed, "is called Capel Coch Road. Keep on it and around the first bend you'll come to Capel Coch. It'll be facing you." I thanked her and then almost ran the length of Capel Coch road and around the bend. There it was right in front of me; this massive non-conformist chapel with its three arched entrances at the tope of some splendid stone steps. I walked up the steps looking neither to the left not to the right in case I should break some awful spell. It was only after I had reached the middle entrance that I turned my head slowly to the left. There was no white-stone grave. In fact, there were no graves of any kind. I hastened to the back of the chapel and there was not a single grave in sight there either. It was all grassland. I was bitterly disappointed. I even began to wonder if my old friend Elwyn could have played a most cruel practical joke on me. But of course, I knew he wouldn't have; not my trusted friend Elwyn.

I knew for certain at this point that whatever the reason there was something macabre about the information we had been given by the nurse spirit in the little front parlour of the council house the previous night. When I arrived at the main entrance of Capel Coch, to be so bitterly disappointed, I knew this was in some way a carefully planned jape. It was just as

31

if the little nurse who had been so willing to provide information and so deliberate in the way she gave it, had given us a right set of clues for us to follow but that for some unknown reason, the 'odd' clues were true and the 'even' clues were false. I found afterwards that Llanberis was one of the few villages in Wales that did not have its own burial place. Llanberis buries its dead in the neighbouring village of Nant Peris, two miles away.

Weeks later, with the mystery still unsolved, I told my expert friend Winnie Marshall about my bewildering experience. She looked me in the eye and then with a twinkle of her own, half-smiled and said: "Well you know Aelwyn, you and your friend Elwyn have been overdoing it just a bit recently. You have been going the rounds boasting how good you are at tackling ghost problems. What did you say in your last book? Was it ninety per cent success you have been having?"

"And you think that a bunch of them on the other side have ganged up together to have their own back on us Winnie?" I asked.

"Since you ask," Winnie chuckled, "that's exactly what I do think. I can well imagine the day you stood on the top step of Capel Coch trembling with excitement, turning your head to look for the suicide grave, a whole lot of spirits rolling around laughing at the trick they'd played on you."

Her explanation at the time seemed so far fetched and so inconceivable. But with hindsight I tend to think she may have been right; and probably was. I have always thought of

Winnie as a person who stands and stares in the other world as much as she stands and stares and observes in this one.

Many years ago she lost a son in a road accident. She told me once that she never once grieved over him. "I see more of him now," she had said, "than I would have done had he been still alive, married, and living in Carlisle."

I think I have a very good idea who two of the dearly departed jokers are who so cleverly took the Mickey out of Elwyn and me. But these spirit jokers have also done something else. They have demonstrated that ghosts are not what most of us think them to be.

They are not the rather sad or solemn kind of people who smile on very rare occasions and move from place to place with a kind of sedate shuffling movement. No. They laugh and they crack jokes in the Afterlife. After all, there have to be millions of children on the other side, many of them waiting for their parents who are still on 'this' side.

I cannot conceive of a heaven where no children laugh.

I have to admit however, that a good number of ghosts I have met have been rather gormless and uninteresting. They seem to waft about at odd hours carrying out peculiar tasks that only they find useful. When I spend an evening with earth friends I invariably come away having learned something new. I often say of my old friend Gwenno Caffell that one has only to be in her company for five minutes and one comes away having learned something new and interesting. But I can't say this of my spirit friends. Many of them are utterly boring. During a lifetime of associating with ghosts I have gleaned very little direct knowledge from them.

But there is a great wind of change in paranormal interest. We now have a Society for Psychical Research. This is a band of highly intelligent research scholars, masters of various disciplines who meet together to investigate and research questions of the paranormal. Most universities which teach psychology will have a professor of Para-Psychology. Things are on the move.

One could even begin to wonder, as the science grows, whether there will be sufficient numbers of ghosts around for all the new students to study. We do know that medical students during their medical school training have to have a number of cadavers to study and to practise their surgery on. It could be asked if there will e sufficient spirit cadavers for ghost research students.

I am absolutely certain that there will be no shortage of spirit subjects. If I were to give my estimate of the spirit population flitting in and out of this earth world of ours at any given time it is more than probable that many of my readers would just shut the book and throw it into the waste basket as rubbish; so improbable would my estimate appear to be. The figure would not be in thousands but in millions.

Elwyn and I have long ago come to the conclusion that there isn't a house in Britain without its ghosts. Yet so many of the people who come to us for advice in their predicament begin their story with the worlds: "I'm afraid we've got a ghost in our house." (Ghost in the singular). And Elwyn and

I are always tempted to reply, "You can say that again," because we know that in every haunted house we have visited we have never found a ghost who has to pay single supplement for his stay. In some of the older houses we have come across whole groups of spirits living together; some in Edwardian clothes, others in the garb of Elizabeth I, some dressed in contemporary outfits. They seem to live in layers; groups of different periods appearing to be oblivious of the existence of the rest.

We arrived in one old house whilst a drinks party for a group of young army officers who had fought in the Crimean War was going on. They were having a veterans' get-together before sailing the following day to take up duties in India. Some gave us their names and ranks and these were subsequently checked out as being correct by the curator-archivist of the Royal Welch Fusiliers museum in Caernarfon. There was no doubting it.

When a ghost is making a real nuisance of himself – and as sometimes happens, frightening the children in the house – the 'team' is often called in to admonish the unruly soul. The admonishing takes about ten minutes but finding him amongst the crowd of other ghosts floating around can take a very long time indeed. I remember Elwyn telling me that sometimes looking for the proper ghost could be like sifting through the crowds at Euston Station.

The family will always stay in the room with us while the search is on and Elwyn will report quite casually what he can see. He will say: "I can see a man of about 30 with dark hair…" and the family will by now be brazen enough to shout him down with a: "Oh no! Not that one again!" I often feel that Elwyn is very often able to witness the kind of scene many of us see on television. The football commentator with microphone in hand reporting the match just played and a lot of young football yobs behind him waving their arms and pulling faces at the camera; doing everything possible to get themselves noticed. Some of Elwyn's ghosts very often behave like.

As one would expect, ghosts still think, and often behave, as humans and continue to show human characteristics. Some are shy and bashful and take a lot of persuading before they are prepared to share our séance. Others are show-off extroverts who can't wait to join in. They all still love – and still hate – as they did when they were alive.

I shall never forget a very strong extrovert ghost that in her life lived in the village of Brynsiencyn, Anglesey, at the time of the First World War. In life, she had been a great three-times a Sunday chapelgoer. In death she still retained two great and poisonous hatreds that she had nurtured during her life. One was the hatred of the poor vicar of the Episcopal Church. This was the period of the disestablishment of the Anglican Church in Wales. Lloyd George was the instigator and Lloyd George was her great hero. But she called the poor parish priest all the names under the sun. Amongst other things, she described him as the Pomeranian of the Marquis of Anglesey. The poodle breed of dogs was presumably not known in Anglesey at this time otherwise the poor old man would have been described as the Marquis's poodle.

Strangely, the other pet hate of this ardent chapelgoer was that great non-conformist revival preacher, the Reverend John Williams, Brynsiencyn. She told us how she used to worship in this man's chapel. But this was until the war broke out and this man, who dared call himself a 'man of God' put on the King's uniform and became an army recruiting officer; "taking blood money for every young lad he could find to send to their deaths in the trenches."

When her minister became a recruiting officer she took to walking miles to the next village to worship her Maker. I met her 50 years after she had died and her hatred towards these two people was just as vile and putrid then as it must have been before her death. I wish somehow that I had never met this lady. I had always hoped that anger, and hatred, jealousy and bitterness were things that faded within us as we grew older and would continue to fade as we proceed through our new life in the next world. But her hatred was still venomous. It is something I still can't understand.

The science of parapsychology is still too young to have its own mathematical and its own geometrical theorems. It has, as yet, no such proven calculus as: "In the right angled triangle the square on the hypotenuse is equal to the sum of the squares on the other two sides."

I only know of one theorem, or one constant, that can be attributed to ghostology and it is:-

> "No spirit can re-enter the earth place without the help of at least two mediums. One medium on the other side to release him and one medium on this side to open the door the receive him..."

37

They do say, but I have no idea who 'they' are, that one in four of all humans are psychic. I don't mean psychic like Elwyn Roberts and Winnie Marshall are psychic – they are the ones who have welcomed this gift and strengthened it by constant use. But the vast majority of those who have the psychic gift don't even know that they have it – although the signs are often there. These are often the people who open their newspapers in the horoscope page every morning. They tell you that their mothers were very good at telling fortunes with tea leaves or that people used to say that their great-grandfather was a gypsy. There is an old aunt somewhere who was possibly good at healing and one relative was reputed to have a peculiar foresight for catastrophes yet to happen. I would be prepared to bet that before the awful disaster of September 11th in New York, it would have been foreseen by a good number of people all over the world. They would probably not have told anyone about their premonitions for fear of being wrong, and if mentioned, their vision after the event they would probably be accused of making it all up.

These are the one out of every four of the world's population who are supposed to be psychic. Most of them have no idea that they are, and if told so would probably forcibly deny it. But nevertheless, they each possess sufficient psychic power, whether they know it or not, to be able to open the door to the visiting spirit from beyond who is anxious to come back to earth and have a little peep at us.

I remember Elwyn, Winnie Marshall and I being invited by council house tenants to visit their home because it had a ghost of a strange man who had his head bandaged and who looked sad and who, they said, managed to infuse his sadness into the house and make the rest of the family sad. It was a simple job. Elwyn and Winnie were both able to focus quite easily on the sad man with the bandaged head. Neither could understand a word he said because he was speaking in a language neither of them was familiar with. Somehow, we were able to work it would that he was talking in Russian. Weeks later, I was able to discover how it came about that a Russian domiciled himself – and met his death – in a small village in the Ogwen Valley of North Wales. The story attracted the national newspapers and was even reported in many of the American press. It was one of those open and shut ghost-hunting stories. Everything fitted into place so very tidily.

And yet when the family left the village some time later the new tenants were asked by the villagers if they had seen anything in their new house. When they reported that they hadn't, many came to believe that the ghost-ridden family must have made it all up otherwise the new tenants would have had the same experiences as they had had.

But not so! True, the Elwyn-Aelwyn team does not go round like *Rentokill* handing out twenty-year guarantees, but we do expect the spirits in the houses we visit to cool their activities after we have been. But in this particular case, the reason the secondly family was unable to see or feel the presence of a ghost was simply that not one of them belonged to the 1-4 group which is psychic enough to open the door for this or any other ghost to enter. This little family could go through life without having ever seen or felt a ghost or until such time, perhaps, as on the girls married a psychic lad or, again perhaps, took in a psychic lodger.

I know of a certain students' Halls of Residence which, at the beginning of a new academic term, suddenly become 'haunted'. Even the tough members of the mens' rugby team fled their rooms in the middle of the night and a whole dormitory wing of the hostel became a no-go area. Investigations showed that that particular year one of the freshers, quite unknown to himself, was a potent sensitive and quite unwittingly it was he would had opened the door to this horrible, witch-like ghost that had taken over the building. And so the theorem rings true. Always, before a spirit can manifest himself on earth there has to be a medium or sensitive on the other side to help, and a second earth medium or sensitive on earth to open the door for him to enter our world.

When one is called to a house and finds that a troublesome ghost is grandma and that she has been dead for 20 years before making her presence known to the family a month ago, one begins to wonder. Has she been waiting for 20 years for one of her non-psychic family to open the door? What new thing, what change in family, happened that made it possible for her to gain entrance after twenty years. There always seems to be a sensible answer.

There is one ghost characteristic that I cannot emphasis enough. Ghosts in general are as reasonable as any representative crowd of humans would be. During the last few years I have had to cut down considerably on house visits. But desperate phone calls still persist. I have had to devise a sort of DIY kit for many that are troubled. I tell them all to wait patiently for the right moment to make contact with their ghostly visitor. Wait until they are on their own in the house. If then they feel the cold air or the rustle that they associate with presence of their ghost, they summon the courage to speak to it. Ask it: "Who are you?" "How can I help you? If you think that I can't help you will you please go away from the house. We are afraid of you and we are all terrified that one of the children will see you and be frightened. This is our house so please go away." I have every confidence that my DIY kit works. In the last two years I have had a good number of my new friends tell me that it does. Like medical GPs Elwyn and I have found that 'home visits' are not as essential as they were deemed to be in the olden days.

If only I could persuade those people who are so terrified of ghosts that ghosts don't always hurt people, that I have never heard of anyone being physically hurt by a ghost. The chances are that the ghost who has settled down in some odd corner of your home is really your own grandfather, or perhaps a great-grandfather who has taken over his own chair once again. In the great majority of cases, the ghost will be family kith and kin. They have no desire to break your bones with sticks and stones.

Note Bene

I have said in this chapter that memory is seated in the physical brain. It is fair, therefore, to ask; if the brain ceases at death, how can spirits still remember where they lived and who their relations on earth were.

Bill Gates, the computer guru, was faced with a similar problem. When an old computer gives its final crash and is beyond repair, it still retains within its hard-drive the knowledge and information it will have collected over the years. Before the old computer is finally committed to oblivion this information is preserved on a floppy-disc and later transferred on to the new machine. I don't understand these things but I would suggest that God would have figured out something along similar lines, although possibly a trifle more subtle so that all the knowledge and experience from earth life is taken from the dying brain and transferred to the mind that continues.

I'm certain that what Bill Gates can do, God can do better.

Chapter Two

<u>**MY GUIDE**</u>

I was brought up a cradle-Christian. With so many evangelical, new-born or born-again Christians around I find the 'cradle Christian' handle just a bit of a handicap.

For all my new-born Christian friends seem anxious to know when exactly I first saw Jesus, and how did I receive my call to the ministry. I'm unable to answer their questions in a way they would understand. I was called to the ministry all right, but I think I would rather die than admit to my new-born Christian friends how.

We had my grandmother living in our house, my mother's mother. Most families of that era had a 'live-in' grandmother and in those days many homes had two - paternal and maternal. I was very fond of my grandmother. She would sit in her rocking chair with a paisley shawl round her shoulders, a lace bonnet adorning her head, and a bottle of Burgundy wine fiercely guarded under her chair for her nightly tipple. When I was about six or seven years old and when we were alone together, she would ask me; "and what are you going to be when you grow up my boy?" I would give a variety of answers: engine driver, policeman, fireman; whatever the whim of the day was and Grandma would just say, "Very good. Very good," and get back to her crocheting.

But on one occasion, probably following a pastoral visit by the vicar, I told my grandma that I would like to be a parson. This brought an entirely new reaction. My gran fumbled amongst the multi-cushions of her chair to find her purse. She then extracted a shiny silver sixpence and gave it to me with a pat on the head and said kindly; "Now *that's* a good boy!"

Forever after, like Pavlov's dogs, my response to " ... *what are you going to be when you grow up my boy*?" would always be "a parson nain." And who is there who would be so foolish as to say that God does not - at least sometimes - call men to his service by using small pieces of Lloyd George's ten shilling weekly pension!

God does work in mysterious ways!

But sixpencees apart I enjoyed my church life and as a child growing-up in a television-free era I even enjoyed the multiplicity of Sunday services and the church's programme of weekday activities. I enjoyed all that the church had to offer except possibly the sermons. But choirboys had their own ways of dealing with this kind of boredom. The latest and most coveted cigarette cards would be displayed under the cover of surplices, and marbles were brought out of cassock pockets for exchange and barter. But I have to admit that when the preacher preached about angels and how they played their part in our lives, I would put away the cigarette cards or marbles and listen attentively. And actually, in post Great War childhood days, there was a great deal of preaching and teaching about angels. In Sunday-school we were taught that every single child had his or her own guardian-angel keeping personal watch. It was a comforting thought.

Then suddenly in the 1930's the talk about angels began to peter out. It was after my ordination that I began to wonder if I had imagined all this angel doctrine. But I looked it up and there it was. The 'Ministry of Angels' had throughout the ages played a significant part in the teaching of the Christian, the Jewish, and Muslim churches. An *angel* is described as a supernatural being, intermediate between man and God. The Christian hierarchy has nine orders whose roles are described in great detail in the bible. The Seraphim, Cherubim and Thrones are those who contemplate God and give Him praise and glory; Dominations, Virtues and Powers are angels who regulate the stars; Principalities, Archangels, and Angels are the angels who minister to humanity.

At one time a traditional Christian belief was that not only did every child have a guarding angel but one was allocated to the entire population, adults as well. Even my grandma had one - Guardian Angels to guard, protect and to guide.

But my own Anglican Church has, over the years, been back-peddling, placing less emphasis on the Ministry of Angels than it did in those days when I was a child. This must also be true in the Roman Church otherwise the Holy Father some time ago would not have felt the need reinstate the belief in angels.

Today I will have been ordained for well over sixty years and I still believe in angels, but not, I hasten to stress, the large, superhuman, be-winged kind that are depicted in Bible illustrations. Those are the angels of poets and artists. I believe in the kind that Spiritualists call Spirit Guides. I have to believe in Spirit Guides because I have seen some. I remember talking to my friend Elwyn Roberts who is an ultra-sensitive sensitive. I don't think it was even night-time or getting dark. I'm sure it was mid afternoon. I was talking to him when his face suddenly changed. His head became bald, but with a long black plait running down his back. His upper lip sprouted long thinnish wisps of a black moustache, his skin became yellow, and his eyes slanted, and there before my very eyes stood a typical Chinese gentleman.

"Elwyn," I exclaimed, "you've changed!"

"What can you see?" asked an unperturbed Elwyn as if change of facial features were an every-day occurrence.

"A chinaman!" I said.

"Oh him!" said Elwyn "he's Ham Hoi my Spirit Guide. I had to ask because I've got another guide as well who is an Anglican priest from the 18th Century."

When I was preparing to draft the text for this book I reminded Elwyn of this incident and he said, "Ah yes indeed, they're always popping up. Would you like a drawing of the two of them to illustrate in your book?" He went on to explain; "I was at a meeting in the Spiritualist Church in Colwyn Bay in 1974 and there was a 'sensitive' artist present. I saw him staring at me when I came in, and then he began to scribble on his pad. During the interval he presented me with the drawings of the two of them, your chinaman and the priest. Neither of them has changed a bit since then! The artist's name was Ifor James. I wonder if Ivor James is still around and still drawing pictures of the spirits he can see around him.

But my great moment came some months later when I visited my friend, Winnie Marshall, in Colwyn Bay. Winnie smiled at me when she opened the door as she always did and then she sort of smiled over my left shoulder as, again, she always did when we met. But this time she said to me, "Your father is such a *lovely* gentleman isn't he Aelwyn?"

"You mean you can see my father Winnie?" I queried, somewhat agog.

"Of course I can," she replied "every time you've been here your father's been with you. You *do* know he's your guide don't you?"

I'm glad Winnie told me I had a guide and that that guide was the father whom I had loved. Since Winnie told me this I have had quite a number of what could have been little guide-like nudges. But I still keep wondering if these little hints and nudges come directly from my guide, or whether they've been prompted from my own imaginings because of what Winnie told me. Winnie assures me not.

This is just one little example of a 'nudge'. I have a tenor voice. Like every good Welshman I harmonise the hymn tunes when I sing in church. I sing the tenor part. But a few Sundays ago I had a cold. I just couldn't reach the tenor notes and so switched to bass. My father had a lovely deep bass voice. I was amazed at just how deep my voice reached on that Sunday morning. It was just as if my father had taken over. Then I tried to persuade myself; "No. You're only thinking this because Winnie Marshall told you that your father was your guide. If she hadn't suggested this to you, you would just have put it down to the fact that you had a bit of a cold and that was why you couldn't reach the high notes."

Point taken. And yet I can't help remembering that this particular hymn, where I was able to round off the bass notes so beautifully and effortlessly, did happen to be my father's most favourite hymn.

During our life together my father had never on any occasion tried to persuade me into any kind of action or decision making. I find it so difficult to believe that my father now accompanies me wherever I go. It is all very well to write and say that other people have guides - but a guide of one's own is a different matter.

But the number of times I have heard friends talk about the kind of activity I think of as guide activity is far too frequent for anyone to explain away simply as coincidence. Typically they say things like: "I didn't go because I had a funny feeling that something awful was going to happen there. I was lucky." Or "Something was telling me all morning that I should go and see my father before we went off for the day. It was a good thing I did. The old man had had a heart attack and the doctor told me that if I hadn't been there at the time the old man would probably have died. We were so very lucky."

Likewise, "I had a hunch that that particular question would crop up during the interview, so I swotted it up. Thank goodness I did, it was a winner!"

I can't agree with them. I don't believe all these hundreds of hunches are sheer luck. To me, these people all seemed to have had competent guides who knew their jobs.

I was delighted to find that my favourite 'media' doctor, Dr James Le Fanu, of the *Sunday Telegraph* seems to agree with me. He appears to have similar ideas about these hunches. He writes: "Chemists seem to be very susceptible to these kind of hunches. Over three-quarters of chemists claimed in a survey to have been guided by a hunch to find the answer to a difficult problem. The essence of a hunch is that it leaps into consciousness, apparently from no where, at a time when a person is doing something else. 'The answer came like a flash one Sunday morning in church while the preacher was announcing his Gospel Text', recalled one of the chemists."

Another described walking down the street, "When suddenly at a definite spot which I could locate today - as if from the clear blue sky above - an idea popped into my head as emphatically as if someone had shouted it."

Dr Le Fanu continues: "The late and great Sir Peter Medawar, a Nobel Prize winner for his contribution to (human organs) transplantation, identified several recurrent features of this type of intuitive inspiration including its suddenness and originality, and, interestingly, that it comes "whole and complete," with an absolute sense of certainty that it must be right. It is just as if the hunch has been communicated directly into the brain by a superior intelligence says Sir Peter.

Dr Le Fanu reports how the famous German pharmacologist, Otto Loewi, woke one night with the brilliant idea of how to prove the existence of the all important neurotransmitters involved in the transmission of impulse from one nerve to the other and whose modification is so important in the treatment of illnesses such as Parkinson's and depression.

He wrote it down on a sheet of paper, which to his consternation, he was quite unable to decipher the following morning. He went to his laboratory hoping that when surrounded all by his equipment, he would be able to make sense of what he had written. But despite frequently taking the paper out his pocket and studying it nothing came. Blanks all day. He retired to bed that night still convinced he must have had a powerful moment of revelation now lost, only to be woken, to his great joy with precisely the same flash of insight which this time he recorded legibly. In the laboratory that morning he performed one of the simplest, neatest and most definitive experiments in the history of biology, confirming the chemical mediation of nerve impulses ... for which, 15 years later, he was duly rewarded with the Nobel Prize.

At the end of that fascinating story I would venture to suggest to Dr Le Fanu that these chemists seem to have been blessed with more powerful guides that the rest of us. Would it be possible that this great pharmacologist, Otto Loewi, could have had either Lister or Pasteur as his guide waking him up at night, or possibly the two of them working together?

Spirit Guides are different from ghosts. One can talk to ghosts and listen to what they are saying. It is even possible to smell ghosts. But spirit guides are different. They don't always show themselves; they keep well in the background. They seem disciplined to do a job and they do it in a professional way. But I have a feeling that spirits alter their practise to suit the circumstances.

The Good Lord has been good to me and to my family. We have six children, 20 grandchildren and one great grandchild and yet neither I, nor they, have been called upon to suffer any *great* stress in our lives. Not the awful stresses that some little families have to endure. We have all been able to enjoy relatively calm lives. And because of this our guides have had few occasions when they have had to come forward and help. I have a theory that when one's life on earth is happy and unstressed the spirit guide places the ship on autopilot and lets it drift. "Steady as she goes." But stresses in life are like storms at sea. The pilot must not only be up on the bridge but he must be seen to be on the bridge. If ever you meet a man who is absolutely certain, without a shadow of doubt, that he has a spirit guide and that he knows how that guide has helped him in his life ask him if he has had a stressful life.

I think you will find that he has.

Chapter 3

<u>Guides Under Stress</u>

So, let me believe that my dear father has been my guide or, shall we say my imagined guide. So gentle and so meek as to be hardly recognisable as a Spirit Guide. He's the sort of guide one would expect a person who had not known great stress in life to have. If we now give the stress screw a quarter turn, and examine the experiences of other people who have suffered real stress in their lives, we would possibly meet the more active, more vibrant, kind of Spirit

Guide. We will come across what is often referred to as a *Crisis Guide*, or a *Crisis Apparition*.

In his book on bereavement my friend, Dr. Dewi Rees describes how he interviewed more than three hundred widows, many of whom had lost their husbands whilst still young. Women who had lost their husbands - many of them suddenly, others after a long illness - could, I think, be described as women who had suffered stress; or who certainly passed through a crisis in their lives. If there are such beings as Spirit Guides these women would have been in need of their support at this time. The same, presumably, is obviously true of bereaved men; but for purposes of this example I'll focus on Dr. Rees's study of widows.

And indeed a great majority of the widows Dr. Rees interviewed did speak of the ghosts, or apparitions, that had come into their lives after they had lost their husbands.

These are the testimonies of some of these women interviewed by Dr. Rees:

"If something crops up I feel him very close and I am guided by him." (Three years widowed)

"It is a sacred thing. I feel there is some nearness, he hasn't actually gone out of my life. I am never afraid." (Three and a half years widowed)

"He is here now and I am not a bit nervous or miserable. Whenever I go out, I always want to return home again because he is there. I slept from the first night he was buried." (Eight years widowed)

"There is nothing like it. It is worth all the money in the world to me. I am very happy and I never feel alone" (Ten years widowed)

"I feel he is with me and looking after me. Before he died I was always terrified of going upstairs, and wouldn't go without a light. Since he died I don't mind going upstairs one little bit. (Eleven years widowed)

"I fancy that if I left here I would be running away from him. Lots of people wanted me to leave but I couldn't. I often hear him walking about. He speaks quite plainly. He looks younger now, more like he was when he was all right, never as he was when he was ill." (Nine months widowed)

I would suggest that it is perfectly obvious that these ladies were not merely telling us about ghosts and apparitions. Had it been just an ordinary ghost, I feel quite certain the poor widow, who had been so afraid of going upstairs in the dark, would have fled for her life. These women are telling us they believe their dead husbands had returned to them; and one of them said, in so many words, that in a crisis he was guiding her. They may never have heard of the term Spirit Guide, but it is spirit guides, nevertheless, they are describing. My guide, and the guides of all other unstressed persons, is ever so faint; they are grey, characterless, figures. The guides of these women who have been under stress are so much stronger and more vibrant and more dominant. It certainly seems that the greater the stress a person has to suffer the greater too the strength given to that person by his guide.

War seems to bring more stress into the lives and accounts of battles fought, traumas suffered and the vivid recollections of more individuals than any other situation. War stories seem to abound with incidents where the guides have actually manifested themselves to those whom they were sent to protect. 'Bob' of The Parachute Regiment was at the very ebb of his endurance when his *'Red Beret'* guide came to his rescue.

Bob's Story.

This incident happened during the 1982 South Atlantic war - the Falklands War - at the height of one the most ferocious battles in modern warfare; the assault to clear Mount Longdon of enemy positions in advance of the main thrust to Stanley.

As our hero is still a member of The Parachute Regiment and has his reputation to keep amongst the younger 'Red Berets,' I'll refer to him only as ... Bob.

By the time Prime Minister Margaret Thatcher despatched the Task Force to the Falklands, Bob had already proved himself in a number of escapades around the world. He and his mate, (and again for the same reason I will disguise his identity by calling him Dave), joined The Paras at Browning Barracks, Aldershot, at the same time. Throughout their careers, from basic training, through recruit selection and 'P' Company and through umpteen tours in Ulster and elsewhere, they had been inseparable pals; sharing everything which soldiers share, their likes, their fears, and their inner-thoughts. They were buddies in every sense; inseparable friends. Professional soldiers.

To say that Bob was a tough, no-nonsense, "hard man" would be an understatement. After the bitter fighting in Goose Green earlier in the campaign he would need all his stamina and all his resilience to pull through the demands which would be made on him on Mount Longdon. But that's what The Paras do best. This was to be a close-quarters battle. Hand-to-hand fighting of the kind not seen since World War II was anticipated - and used. It was a gruesome, and even by Para standards of endurance, terrifying.

Contemporary regimental chronicles of the events openly admit there was mayhem. It was dark, men were rushing through, and others were backtracking with stretcher-borne causalities. Young inexperienced officers sat sobbing; their older NCO's taking control. The noise was deafening.

In the height of battle Bob missed his bearings and became detached from the main group. Then 50 metres ahead of him he caught sight of a nest of Argentinean 'machine-gunners'. He instantly raised his weapon. The slightest squeeze on the trigger of his rifle would have released a burst of certain slaughter. But in that split second, as his eye lined the rifle sight, it wasn't the blurred outline of the Argentinean position he saw in front of him. He saw now the fully upright, almost larger-than-life frame of his old mate Dave. Dave with his arms held high, in the recognised surrender position, screaming above the cacophony of background noise of mortar, machine gun and artillery fire: *"Not now Bob! Not Now! HOLD YOUR FIRE!"*

But even his adrenaline-racing mind told him Dave had no business to be anywhere near the Falklands. Dave had been killed in Northern Ireland some years earlier. Yet there he was, larger-than-life, in the webbing and Para-gear used in Ulster during the 1970's; shouting at Bob to hold his fire

The shock was enough to jerk Bob's rifle upwards; a round of 7.62mm exploded upward into the night air. By the time Bob re-sighted Dave was gone - as quickly as he had appeared. It had been a hard few days. Bob was tired; he was exhausted. It could have been a trick of fatigue or of nerves. He re-sighted his weapon but this time with a little more caution. Maybe the Para he had seen a moment ago was Dave, maybe it wasn't. What certainly. was true, however, was that the machine gun nest he had assumed to be Argentinean wasn't Argentinean at all. It was a group of three British soldiers, an artillery forward-observer, a radio operator and an infantryman who had flanked away from the main attack and into enemy lines and who were calling in fire onto Argentinean positions.

Bob lowered his sights, he looked around for Dave - or Dave's Parachute Regiment look-alike - but no one was to be seen. To this day he is happy to tell this tale. A *'blue-on-blue'* had been averted. Dave, his old mate, had fleetingly revisited Bob as his Guide … or perhaps the *guide* to three lucky British soldiers, who, through Dave, had escaped death by seconds.

Bob was later to recall the pre-battle briefing which 3 Para's Company Sergeant Major Johnny Weeks had given the men in the moments before the battle of Mount Longdon:-

"Gentlemen," CSM Weeks had said *"You're to have things happen to you that you have never experienced before when you were training. If any of you believes in Christ, here's the time to sit down and have a little talk with Him. It's not stupid. I'm just off now to have my little prayer."*

And something, which had never happened to Bob in seven years of soldiering, happened to him at this time. Bob – this tough, hard-nosed, member of Britain's elite Airborne Forces discovered his God - he now leads a life of prayer.

There is nothing very new about these tales of War Guides. It is said that even Napoleon and Wellington, in their separate camps, relied quite a lot on their respective war guides, and of course the World War I appearances of *The Angels of Mons* are now legend.

Touched by and Angel: the story of a drowning helicopter pilot.

Heathrow-based pilot Captain Richard Ball – a family friend – flies long-haul jets around the world. He began his flying career as an S-61N helicopter pilot, firstly for Bristow Helicopters in the North Sea, later as a police helicopter pilot and eventually as one of the personal aviators of King Fahad of Saudi Arabia.

Credentials over.

Richard was therefore particularly keen to read-up and listen to every last scrap of information about the sea-crash suffered by two colleagues flying and aircraft identical to his old Sirkorski S-61N, (this aircraft is the civilian equivalent of the RAF and Navy's search and rescue helicopter, the *Sea King*).

The technical report after the crash, published by the CAA Air Accident Branch ran into thousands of words. Copies appeared in thick dossiers and in précis form on crew room noticeboards. They were essential reading for the plane makers, maintenance engineers, safety executives, air accident investigators, insurers and underwriters. Richard's interest as a pilot, who at the time was flying a similar type helicopter over the most hostile waters around Britain and Norway was perhaps less technical. He simply wanted to know how the crew and passengers had escaped; how they'd coped

The helicopter would have gone down quickly. There would have been little or no opportunity to activate the well-practised procedures other than for transmission of a '*Mayday*'. The crew of two pilots would have been almost demented in their effort to do the best they could for their 18 passengers and their flight attendant who would all have been strapped into their seats behind the flight-deck. Past training would have taught them that their own safely should come last. Even as the aircraft began to submerge there were 'shut down' procedures to complete.

And when a shuddering eight-tonne helicopter, laden with passengers, luggage, cargo and a full load of fuel suddenly drops from the sky into the sea, it certainly doesn't land like confetti on a millpond. It plummets.

Cabin lights failed, the sea burst in, there was the mayhem of human screaming, the rush of noise as the still-turning rotor blades and gears battle against water turning it into a froth of black mush. The Captain and his First Officer now some twelve feet down and still sinking fast. would know that their next, urgent responsibility would be to swim out of the flight deck to unlock the starboard door, unleash the heavy on-board liferaft, and guide their passengers to the surface and survival.

But as the machine hit the water it had turned at least once, then corkscrewed, and could possibly have turned again. It was black dark. Lungs were already screaming for air; the Jacuzzi of foaming air bubbles gave no clue as to where they would rise, or if the helicopter was upside down, where they would 'fall'. There were no telling tale air pockets to be seen. The natural instinct would be to swim 'upwards' – to the surface. But having been trained in simulated survival techniques in deep water tanks they knew that in the blackness of a rolling, sinking helicopter how difficult it was to plot which way 'upward' is to the surface. It was their job to find it and to guide their passengers to safely out of the door and the escape hatch at the side of the aircraft.

It was then, in this horrible dilemma – seconds possibly from drowning – that a *"sense of absolute calm and warmth"* came over one of the two pilots. There were no audibly whispered spirit guide voices saying *'follow me'*; no mirages of signs saying 'Swim left'. But it was *'like the presence of an angel* ' described this pilot later. He said the angel, who touched him calmed him, slowed his racing heartbeat, and focused him on to the route he, his colleagues, and a full manifest of passengers should take to safety. Every single person on that aircraft survived.

My friend Richard certainly knew the identities of the two brave helicopter pilots who fought their controls and the physics of gravity, who experienced the confusion of disorientation, and who then fought to save their passengers before thinking of their own danger. But Richard didn't know which of the two was the one *'touched by an angel* ' or perhaps touched by a spirit guide.

Nor, friend as he is, was he willing to let me approach either of two pilots directly. "Pilots," he said, "are under constant medical, physical and psychological scrutiny. A pilot who claimed that he flew with the guidance of angels and spirits would guarantee for himself a very rapid retirement from the operational fleet; he could expect to be unceremoniously bounced down to some low-risk desk job.

"Strangely though," Richard adds, "we're officially encouraged to formally report sightings of possible UFOs and other unusual phenomena and we do so with some frequency. But anything else which is to do with the paranormal or the supernatural is taboo ... it's a short runway from the shrink's couch and the withdrawal of your licence to fly to the dole queue."

But he never doubted for one moment the truth of his colleague's account of that near-catastrophe experience. And then he said; "Unless you've actually ditched an aircraft into blacked-out, churning, deep waters or you have experienced total disorientation, either flying in cloud with no instruments or sinking into the sea in a rolling, twisting, helicopter, you have no idea how difficult it is to chose which of a possible 360 degrees to choose from. Any of the 359 incorrect options - with lungs already bursting for air will most certainly have taken you to your death."

Whilst researching my book and in attempt to validate the story and expand on it, I wrote a letter to *Flight International*, the world pilots' bible, asking if there was anyone who could tell me more about this amazing incident. They didn't reply and they didn't publish my letter. This confirms Richard's view. Report UFOs by all means, but let's hear nothing about the 'hand of God' and the work of his angels.

And that is a pity

Still, hope springs eternal. The pilot who was touched by an angel is by now undoubtedly retired or at least, past the age of promotion. His pension is secure. I would love to hear this account from his own lips. It is such an amazing story that tells how one man was able to lead 20 others to safety from near or almost certain death - and to hear from him at first hand how, at the end, it wasn't solely him that controlled matters – it was the angel who touched him.

Colonel, Guide, and Desert Rats

I remember a friend of mine telling me about his experiences as one of Monty's Desert Rats in the 8th Army. He told me that when Monty moved his army in the desert he would always twist and turn his convoys. Monty would hardly ever go in a straight line. But he added, "Mind you, we had to hand it to the old chap that whenever we did come to a halt the Sappers would always find a good supply of water." He explained that there was never enough for every man to have a make-shift shower but there would be enough to enable each man to replenish his ration of half a pint a day. And half a pint a day, per head, for a whole army was a lot of water to have to find in the parched North African desert.

Then you have to add the number tanks, tank-transporters, 10-tonners, field-guns, Jeeps and other machines that also had to be topped up. It appears that Monty's turning, and twisting, and detouring, over many miles in his search and battle confrontations with Rommell, was done almost always on receipt of a coded signal from the War Office in London. It always seemed to happen that in the most uncompromising and parched *waddis*, they would find underground water wells. Rommell apparently didn't enjoy the same 'field intelligence' as to the source of this critical supply. The fact is that not even Monty himself, nor his intelligence officers, knew how the boffins that were cosseted in the War Office in London, came up with such precise water knowledge. Monty's locally employed and indigenous *Bedouin* trackers were equally dumbfounded. They knew how to find water in areas within a 60 miles radius of their own villages but not,

Inshallah (God Praise be Willing) across the entire North African continent.

My old friend who told me the story didn't care how the water was found; neither probably did his old co-gunner Spike Milligan. Sufficient to know that when the 8th Army needed water *Allah* always seemed willing to provide. But Allah provided for British troops only. It was long after the end of World War II, under the government's 30-Year Secrecy Rule, that my friend's curiosity was satisfied.

It appears that throughout the desert-war and in a War Office requisitioned country mansion outside Oxford there existed a formidable two-man team. A team more powerful than the more modern ones armed with war-technology satellites, seismic loggers, geohydro sensors and geo-scientific instruments. One of the duo was a Lieutenant Colonel in the Royal Corps of Engineers; the other - never decorated for his 'war effort' or even formally de-mobbed on war pension - was his *Spirit Guide.*

The Lieutenant Colonel and his faithful guide would pore over battered field-maps of North Africa, many of them unchanged since the days of Gordon of Khartoum. Void of any geological data, absent of any meaningful geographic contours save for the occasional dry well or the dotted line of a camel track, they were pretty useless charts. They might as well, the two of them, have sat and peered at blank sheets of paper.

In my earlier book, "*Holy Ghostbuster,*" I made reference to divining; otherwise known as dowsing, that inexplicable ability some of us have to divine water using a hazel branch or with a metal coat hanger. Here in the early 1940's, in a pipe-smoked dining room of an old Oxfordshire country home thousands of miles from the North African desert, a Royal Engineer Colonel and his spirit guide worked that paranormal divining magic to find water holes large enough to quench the thirst of Monty's Desert Rats. The task was formidable. Brigades, Divisions … a whole Army of water-thirsty men and machines had to be constantly watered.

Military buffs will know the story well. In the old Colonel's obituary in the *'Daily Telegraph'* a few years ago the story was given a rather inconsequential and cursory mention. These things, not being the science of war, *'don't come up to muster'* as the top-brass would say. But to those of us who wish to know more about spirit guides the story goes a bit like this:

Each day, a motor bike despatch-rider would race from the War Office in Whitehall to Oxfordshire with Monty's latest "Secret" battle plans for The 8th Army. These plans would have been approved in the War Office. The army of men, tanks, lorries, jeeps, artillery and supporting vehicles would need to consume thousands of gallons of water *en route* to Monty's next battlefield. None was shown on available maps; and those water holes or bores that did exist could be assumed to have been contaminated by the enemy's Afrika Korps.

Maps of the next battle attack and the route it would take would be carefully laid out on the large table in the old country house in Oxfordshire. The Royal Engineers lieutenant-colonel and his spirit guide would lock minds. The colonel would use a large pencil instead of the traditional hazel twig; the guide would lead his hand. "X" marks the spot so to speak.

Our good colonel apparently had no natural talent for water divining. He tried it years later and was an abysmal failure. However, his spirit guide certainly did have a talent for finding water. He probably couldn't paint, or play the piano to save his life; he was just a champion water-diviner. He could have said to the old colonel, "Here my dear friend, I can help you and Mr Churchill and the war effort."

Now there's a strange twist to this tale; one that I find difficult to explain.

Spirit guides - even the most accomplished and knowledgeable - have sometimes to confess ignorance; to having limited information about particular topics only. After Monty beat Rommell in North Africa the War Office concentrated attention on Europe. Churchill planned a fast and ruthless invasion into the heart of the Rhine. The undoubted, but still secret, bond between the colonel and his guide was to be put to a new test. Maps were again needed. The Germans had flooded the Low Countries of Europe and swamped the areas round Normandy. *'Operation Overlord'* and the D-Day invasion were at risk. "Give us intelligence!" screamed the War Office; but this time nothing happened. The Colonel begged and implored but his old guide was impotent and determined to remain so.

Either the guide knew nothing about the geology and geography of Northern Europe or he was limited in his hydro-geological knowledge. Winnie Marshall's guides know how to paint but I doubt if they had a clue how to guide Winnie's hands to do ASME IX welding or trombone playing. Guides too have their limits. This guide's knowledge was either North Africa or water holes. (I wonder if he had been a Bedouin Arab in his first existence!) Ask him to find a swamp in Normandy rather than a *waddi* in Egypt and the poor soul was, pardon the pun, out of his depth - or perhaps he thought his duty done and simply went AWOL!

The Ziggy Bossowski 's Story.

This story came to me from Zbigniew "Bill" Bossowski, who died peacefully of old age in 1998; then aged 85. I had the great privilege of meeting Ziggy – or "Bill" - when at the age of 81 he made a remarkable 50th Anniversary commemorative parachute jump into Arnhem, Holland. For him - as all good Hollywood film scripts insist - his 'war was over' in the carnage which was to be his "*Bridge Too Far*" in September 1944: "Operation Market Garden."

Ziggy was a remarkable soldier.

With due deference to our modern day troops, I would venture to say he was unique. On World War II 'demob' Ziggy found himself entitled to three army pensions in three different rank brackets; Polish Army, Free French Army [fighting with the French Resistance] and the British Army.

He fought his war never knowing what rank he was supposed to hold. Lieutenant in the Polish Army, private in the Free French, rankless in the Resistance and Acting Captain [Adjutant] in the 1st Polish Independent attached to the British Army's 1st Airborne Division. His medals were also very confusing and his battered old grey Polish Airborne beret, which he wore virtually to his death bore many of his earlier identities.

Ziggy was a man who hedged his bets. But on one principle he would not compromise. Ziggy in the 1930s was a "a non-believer." His is a chilling story but one which provides further evidence of the existence of spirit guides. His story confirms for me that Spirit Guides, like God Himself, are omnipresent. They travel widely and are always ready to take action on our behalf when such action is required.

This is the stress-cog now turned to its ultimate.

Despite the all-embracing cloak of Catholicism which ran through Poland in the years before, during and after the war, Ziggy Bossowski remained an atheist. For Ziggy there was no God.

The story of Ziggy is one familiar to my son Mark. Mark and other members of the Army Parachute Association took Ziggy "Bill" Bossowski under his wing in the Arnhem Veteran's return parachute jump in 1994 when 86 remarkable veterans aged between 69 and 86 sky-dived back into the original drop-zone in Holland. The story is also known to Major Bob Card MBE BEM, recently retired as Commandant of the Joint Service Parachute Training Centre, Netheravon, Wiltshire. Major Card is a professional soldier; not known for emotions or small talk, but who will always shed a small tear when recalling the Bossowski story. It is one that Ziggy was equally happy to relate, in old age, to his Arnhem-veteran friend - and brave co-jumper 50 years on – the Reverend Ray Bowers, a surviving airborne padre of The Parachute Regiment's worst battle.

I don't think any book on the subject of Spirit Guides would be complete without reference to Ziggy's account; an account only related to his closest 'airborne' friends; my son being among them.

Ziggy was a young officer in the Polish army when the Germans invaded and overwhelmed his country. Facing a devastating defeat as the German tanks advanced on Warsaw, Ziggy was ruthless in his killing of occupying German soldiers. Like others, hoping for the early liberty of their country, he became more and more adept in the art of close-quarters fighting and killing his enemy.

However he and five other Polish fighters were arrested and handed over to the local Gestapo. To their number was added 18 other non-combative villagers – 'peasants'. Ziggy described them as men who'd been arrested for no other reason than that they were in the wrong place at the wrong time. Two days later with horrendous wounds inflicted by brutal torturing and beatings, he and his non-combative companions were marched to the local Town Hall and placed against its wall. They were to face a firing squad.

Let me now tell Ziggy's story of what happened next. This is the story he told my son and has subsequently been verified by his own contemporaries. His story is for real. His Spirit Guide is also for real. These are his words:

"We wanted to march to the wall with some dignity but we could only shuffle. Old men, young men, some who couldn't see through the puss and the swelling of their eyes; others with broken bones, others just broken completely.

"We thought maybe its OK. The fight is over. Stand there, wait a minute, then *bang*, and it's all over. But you know, you don't think like that, even though you are thinking everyone else is thinking like that. You are like jelly.

"We come to the wall. We turn. It is not like the films. No posts, no blindfold, no last cigarette - just turn to face the rifles. You cannot focus. There is no fear, just worry about how you will react in front of your friends - and jelly legs.

"I don't want to look but I have to turn and see where my friends are. How do they face their death? Like me? Nervous? I turn my head. Next to me there is a priest. Where did he come from? He was not walking behind me to the wall. His face is smiling; but not smiling. A sort of calm smile that isn't a smile, but is. This man is at peace. It cannot be explained. He is not looking at me but he is talking to me and only to me. He says; "Put your chest out. Look ahead. I will be with you now and tomorrow. You are with me." Then he smiles. This is a real smile. I look ahead and heave my chest. I am drunk in my head not knowing what to think. Think about being shot or think about where the priest came from. I wish I had time to think about both things at the same time.

"I look again to my left, quickly now as the soldiers raise their weapons. He is still standing there. But there is no order to 'SHOOT '

"Instead, a young German officer rushes forward - almost running - he is shouting and excited. There is a panic somewhere in the town. There is no time for executions today. The execution is postponed. The SS guard have better things to do than waste bullets on peasants and time cleaning up the mess he says. We are marched back to our cells - until tomorrow. I turn to the left to shuffle back again, but there is no priest. Just an old man I knew from the village. The priest is gone!"

Ziggy's memory of it was as if it was yesterday. He continued: "But tomorrow never came. The priest did and in a way I cannot tell you how. With him I walk away from my captors - escape - and he is walking behind me. No one else escapes. He is with me as I make escape through Austria and into France. He is with me sometimes two times every day, sometimes gone for a week. Then I join the French Resistance.

"Again I am caught. This time I think, "Ziggy you have run out of luck" I know that SS in France will telephone to Gestapo in Poland, and the Gestapo in Poland will say: *"Aa-ha, you have Ziggy Bossowski - he make fool of us*!

"I think maybe I should pray, but I have never made prayer before. I have never said to God "Thank you God" so

72

why now I say to God "Please help me God"? We are in a room in a French schoolhouse with guards. I am frightened now. In Poland I am with friends as firing squad takes aim. Now I am going to be alone without friends.

"Then he comes again. This is the priest I see in Poland. He is not changed; still in his drab clothes. He is still with a look that says 'no problem', and a smile that says trust him. 'It's OK' he says.

"Next day I am marched to a military vehicle. It is cold. I am frightened. I am still only young you know. Soldiers say we are all going back to Poland. The truck drives for maybe 150 kilometres towards Dijon and the North East. They stop on a hillside to let us go for a pee. In the hill high above me is the priest. The same smile but he is not talking. But I know what he is saying. He is saying for me to get my head down and stay down. Then there is shooting from the woods. They are the French Resistance. The Germans run for their vehicles, re-mount and drive off quickly. I'm alone. Everyone else scatters – *vermoosh*! The priest is gone. I still do not pray to God but I know I should. Again I have escaped.

"Four months later I am in England and have joined Polish Independent Parachute Brigade. We are going to Arnhem in Holland. The biggest airborne drop ever.

British soldiers parachute-jump on September 17th. but the weather makes it impossible for Polish Independent Airborne to land until two days later. By then all the SS Panzer Division know that we are coming and where we will land.

They wait for us in the woods around the Drop Zone and are opening fire. It is murder as we drop over Holland. But again I am lucky. I cannot see him now, and I cannot hear him, but I know that my priest is in Arnhem too. And he is with me on the long march to Germany after we are captured, and in the train wagons that take us east to Stalug P.o.W. Camp.

"I did not see him after we arrive safely at the camp. Perhaps because I am no longer in danger. He had delivered me to safety. Then I begin to pray every day to say "*Thank you God*.""

None of those who ever knew Ziggy Bossowski - my son included - had ever had any doubts that the Polish priest, who stood shoulder-to-shoulder mentoring Ziggy as he lined up for execution in Poland, was arrested with the French Resistance, fought bravely in Arnhem, was recaptured again, and who, 50 years later, made a spectacular freefall tandem parachute jump at speeds peaking 130 mph from 17,000 feet, was not with him to the end.

In any case Ziggy Bossowski smoked 60+ cigarettes a day and drank like a fish until his death at the age of 85.

His priest had to have been with him … or he'd have had to have been born a cat.

It would have been nice to think that all these war fighting Guides were given the highest gallantry medals. Perhaps, of course, they're already wearing them in the Officers' Mess known as *Summerland*!

Chapter Four

A Guide in Disguise

I found this lovely but somewhat disturbing story waiting for me on my *website* one Saturday evening.   I had previously advertised that I would be pleased to hear from anyone who had had experience of spirit guide activity.

This story of a very peculiar spirit guide came from Colin. No surname and no address, just his *e.mail* and a little introductory note to say that he had never before told of his experience to another person; it seemed to him so ridiculous.

He felt my 'web' appeal could be a "No name no pack drill" way of unburdening himself of something he had mulled over for a very long time. The anonymity of my website being, perhaps, like a catharsis. Other people might talk to the Samaritans or their parish priest. His release was to write down his experience,

Colin at the time of the incident had his own business in London. He was his own boss; his business had been flourishing. He was amongst the thousands of people who caught the same crowded commuter train into the City every day and joined the same throngs to the same crowded train every evening for the homeward rush. He had a wife, three young children and a lovely home to come back to every evening.

Things had gone well for many years. Then all of a sudden something had gone wrong. I couldn't quite understand how, but he intimated that it was something to do with the collapse of the *dot.com* industry in 2001. Profits had suddenly collapsed. His company now barely made enough money to pay the office rent or his commuter season ticket. There was also a debt - a large debt. Jean, his wife, would have to be told of course, and the news would soon have to be broken to the children. How do you explain to young children that the mortgage couldn't be paid and that they'd have to move to a smaller house in a less affluent area.

This Friday evening he had stayed longer than usual at his desk. He had cleared it, shredded the waste and had packed all his files neatly. He called into a local wine-bar to take final stock of his position and then caught a bus to London

Underground's Blackfriars Station for the connection to Waterloo. He'd purposefully timed it so as to avoid the six o'clock rush. The first of the evening commuter exodus was over and the second, the West End theatre-goers had not yet begun. Tonight he really would have to tell Jean. Jean would understand, but why the hell should she. All this had been his own doing. Jean and the children were just the victims of his mismanagement in not predicting the collapse of the industry he depended on. The responsibility was his, the unpaid debts were his. He was an encumbrance to his family. They would manage very well without him - better without him than with him in actual fact. He was a burden to them. There would be state benefits. Jean had already sold a good number of her water-paintings. She had lots of friends and her parents were only 15 miles away. They would manage very well without him. I could imagine what was coming next.

At this point – now in the emptiness of Blackfriars Station - he found himself looking up to where each of the underground's CCTV cameras had been placed on the station platform. After years of travelling the same route, he knew them all. The sign above advised the next westbound train would approach in three minutes. Three minutes to walk out of CCTV range and three minutes to say his quiet goodbyes to himself. He decided that before he did it, he would make the sign of the cross; his last physical action in this world would be the making of the sign of the cross.

It is at the point, where CCTV cameras cease to cover the platform's extreme ends that trains run fastest. Thousands of tons of almost unstoppable train and carriages. He walked to the end of the platform; his eyes now focused on the track lines. He really didn't want to look the train driver in the face.

There below him and between the railway lines he saw a mouse. A little brown mouse that scurried at speed towards him as if from nowhere and then halted mid-track between high voltage lines and the tracks directly beneath him on the platform. It sat on its little haunches, stroked its whiskers and seemed to say; "*Oi! Look at me! LOOK AT ME*!!"

And look at him he did. He shouldn't have been able to penetrate a mouse's eyes at that distance but he could. They were sparkling brown and pleading and Colin kept looking into them, mesmerised. He remembered thinking that at that moment both he and the little mouse were in extreme danger. "Look…at…me! *Please* keep looking at me!" pleaded the unheard voice. "I have no where to go, no food, no family, lost in this hellhole, no escape, trains thundering over me, high voltage lines beneath. But I am surviving … I'll find a way out. And so will you. You MUST find a way out!" It was, Colin described, as if the mouse, of all creatures, knew exactly what torment, anguish and mental suffering Colin was going through.

Anyone who has travelled the London Underground is bound to have seen the occasional mouse trapped in the corridor of tracks. But they will always scurry away as they sense the train approaching through the tunnel; as they feel the blast of warm air approaching and feel the tracks vibrate. They're not daft! "But this one didn't," Colin said, "he just stood upright on his haunches, eyes open and in direct eye-to-eye contact with me throughout. He was still talking and still saying to me "Look at me! Keep looking at me!" It was at this point Colin began to surmise his railway-track mouse as his spirit guide. There was a bonding like super-glue between them. He said, "I remember reading how police negotiators are trained to use the same technique in their mediation with suicide cases, 'Look at me! Keep looking at me!' they say. They are told that once eye contact is lost, the cause is very often lost. This mouse, or spirit-mouse, had obviously undergone the same kind of training!"

The train thundered past and slowed to its halt. With tears of relieved emotion Colin entered a near-empty carriage and finally made his way home. The following day he sought professional help. Colin's story had a happy ending, but it left me with a problem.

This was the first time in my life I had been asked to believe that a spirit guide could take on the form of animal bodies just as they do human bodies. Ziggy 'Bill' Bossowski's guide was a priest, Ziggy was an atheist. Nothing would have shaken Ziggy into action more than the shock of being rescued by a priest. The guide that took the form of a paratrooper in the Falklands might not have been a paratrooper at all, but had taken the form of a paratrooper in order to perform his job. I would accept that it would be possible for a guide to appear in the guise of a priest, soldier, sailor, tinker, spy. But a mouse?

The self-taught ghostology student has to ask if such a thing is feasible? Is it logical? Does it make sense? (When dealing with suicide stories one must always remember that many of those contemplating the taking of their own life are generally regarded as 'those whose balance of mind is disturbed'). But even so when one really thinks about this story the answer to the three questions has to be a reserved 'Yes'.

In this particular context it is feasible, it is logical, and it *does* make sense. Here was a man walking deliberately to a pre-meditated and convenient place to kill himself by throwing himself under a train. There was precision planning. Nevertheless every muscle in his body is rigid, every nerve tense. At this point, even if a Samaritan, priest, police negotiator a station porter or even his wife walked up to him or spoken - he would have jumped. But a little mouse with its piercing brown eyes and its voice that was not a voice shouting, *"Look at me. Look at me ... if I can survive, so can you ... "* was enough to daunt him in his purpose.

If Colin ever comes to read this book of mine I would like him to know that I am not doubting him for a moment. But I'm not, either, saying that I categorically believe that the mouse he saw that night was a spirit-guide in the guise of a mouse. I feel quite sure that men under stress, and who are about to commit suicide, do probably see peculiar and unexplainable things. On the other hand Colin could have been right when he says that he was saved that night by a mouse spirit guide.

I have seen human spirits - ghosts. I have even chatted with these ex-human persons, but I have to confess that I have never actually seen an *animal* ghost. If there was a book written about animal ghosts I have a feeling I could be tempted to break my rule of not reading other people's ghost stories. But animal ghost is still a subject I wouldn't want to become too involved with - the human variety is often more than I can tackle. On the other hand it is a subject I would like to know a little more about.

Animals are certainly more psychic than humans.

Now-retired Chief Inspector Ernie Plumb recounted to me a hair-bristling story of animal 'sensitivity' that he was personally part of in the 1970's while serving with the City of London Police.

The City Police prided themselves with having a dog so ferocious and eager to make arrests that whenever incidents occurred on the boundary with their Met. Police 'patch' Met dogs would cower in submission to the greater build and authority of Bruno. Bruno was a monster. His dog-van would physically shake as Bruno sensed the excitement of a criminal chase or a good sniff.

Bruno was on top form on an October night when the '999' phones began ringing at Old Jewry Police HQ. Havoc was being reported inside an empty pub adjacent to a City of London church off Cheapside. Control Room phones went berserk with the volume of passer-by calls. City Police stood *en-masse* outside the pub waiting for the rocking 'n rolling of the dog-van transporting their brute Bruno. The din coming from inside the building was cacophonic. It was equally loud inside the dog-van as Bruno readied himself for the chase!

Bruno was let off the leash and tore into the building with teeth bared and ears up. Ernie Plumb and his men stayed on the pavement, lit their cigarettes and took side bets on how long it might take before screaming intruders would come rushing out, gibbering and bloodied with Bruno snapping at their heels.

It was, however, Bruno who tore out first … projected like a missile out of a third floor window to the pavement below; yelping and his tail tucked firmly under his hind quarters. No amount of coaxing would get the whimpering, blubbering, Bruno back into the building. He skulked back to his van, shaking violently and curled himself into a pathetic ball under his blanket.

It was now the turn of his human counterparts to enter the building. They, too, exited ashen-faced and traumatised. They witnessed havoc and stench that no human could have created – for there were, indeed, no humans inside and no sign of forced entry. A month later, Bruno was retired from the Force, a broken, pathetic dog suffering from the canine equivalent of Post Traumatic Stress Disorder.

"I don't know what he saw in there," said Ernie, "but I'm certain he didn't just leap out. The force behind his exit from the window was far too powerful.

"Whatever it was must have been awesome. Bruno obviously 'saw' what we couldn't. We could only see the devastation and smell the stench of this revolting 'thing'. I have no doubt that it was a poltergeist of some sort."

I remember many years ago I used to keep and eye on a colleague's vicarage while he and his family were on holiday. He would give me the keys and I would walk round the property two or three times a week during his absence; I would never go in and never use the keys.

On one occasion when I was conducting my caretaking perambulations a car rolled up the drive. It was the family returning home early from their holiday. We exchanged greetings; "Good holiday? What was the weather like?" that sort of thing. My colleague seemed a little impatient of smalltalk. 'Well Aelwyn, we must unpack and get the luggage out of the car." I offered to give a hand; an offer which was politely declined. A strange thing then happened. My colleague went into the car pocket and extracted a small crucifix. Holding the crucifix above his head he opened the Vicarage door and walked in. The rest of the family just sat calmly in the car. It was quite obvious that this action with the crucifix was something they were all well used to. The children probably thought this was something all parsons did when they came home from holiday. In minutes he was back again and the remainder of the family tumbled out of the car and into the house. It was now okey for me to lend a hand. He and I were left to carry the cases from the boot.

I learnt later that during his few minutes away my colleague would have entered every room, crucifix held high, and he would have said a short blessing in every single room in the house, the attic and cellar included.

Months later my friend told me they had a ghost in their house. There were six of them that lived in this rambling old vicarage; the vicar, his wife, their three children, his wife's sister - a young widow - and her child of three. Life went on just as it did in every other home except for a periodic incident that would last for about 15 minutes. These incidents would happen about three or four times a year. My friend added that the incidents had, up to now, occurred in the night after the children had gone to bed so they, the kids at least, knew nothing about them.

The incidents would happen when the three grown ups were in the room together in the late evening. The three of them would be doing their own thing, reading, knitting, writing when suddenly they would all look up to a corner of the room. It was something they would do in concert. It reminded me of the little mouse's, "Look at me! Look at me!" cry on the London Underground. There, in the far corner of the room they would see a huge goat, and the animal would be glowering at them. The goat would remain in the room for up to fifteen minutes and then it would sort of fade away again. I have heard so many similar stories but both the man who was telling me about this particular ghost and his wife were both first class science graduates. They had lived in the Vicarage for five years, so one had to assume that they would have had to put up with the goat experience about 15 to 20 times during their tenure. I asked him about this. He told me he and his wife had managed, in part, to break the spell. They felt a compulsion to look when the thing made its first appearance but after a few minutes they had been able turn away, and return to their reading, or writing, or whatever they were doing, and just glance occasionally to see if it had gone away. In this way by denying the thing the attention it was obviously seeking, they hoped to be able to drive it away. But poor Angela, his sister-in-law, was apparently mesmerised by the thing and stared at it the whole time.

There had been an incident a year previously when Angela and her little girl had not joined them on their summer holiday. They had stayed behind at the Vicarage. They had been away only a few days when the vicar's wife woke up with a start in the middle of the night in their holiday hotel. She told her husband that she would have to telephone her sister Angela. She had the most horrible feeling that something had happened to her. She rang her sister at three o'clock in the morning in spite of her husband's counsel to wait until the morning. But Angela and her little Ann were all right; nothing had happened. Angela hoped they were both having a nice holiday.

It was only after they had returned home that the mystery of the night telephone call was solved. Angela told them, "It was strange," she said, "little Ann and I were both asleep in bed when I woke up with a jerk and there it was, the goat, standing at the foot of the bed. He wasn't making a noise but I knew from his nostrils that he was snorting. I was petrified. It stayed for as long as it usually stays on his down-stairs visits then it then faded away. You rang half an hour later. Fortunately by this time I had had time to get over my shock. I tried to act as naturally as I could; I didn't want to spoil your holiday.

"I knew Morgan would want to come home the next day if I told you we had had a visit - so I said nothing."

Chapter 5

<u>Grand Order of Royal Guides</u>

As far as we know it was after the death of her beloved Prince Albert that Queen Victoria became seriously absorbed in spiritism. This interest continued, and grew, during her long period of widowhood. There seems little doubt that she revered the psychic power of her gillie and confidant John Brown. Over the years when she became known as '*The*

Black Widow' he seemed to have become the earth link with her departed husband Prince Albert. To her Brown could even, in their later lives, have become the reincarnation of her greatly loved husband.

It is known that Victoria, John Brown and certain of her ladies-in-waiting did have long drawn out seances with Brown acting as medium. Questions posed were invariably directed to Prince Albert. What does Albert think of the current bill going through parliament, and what reply might he give to the Prime Minister's latest query about the *Children Act*? Very often her Prime Ministers would be kept waiting for the Queen's ruling in matters parliamentary until Albert - or gillie Brown - had deliberated. These séance sessions were apparently well known within the royal family and the royal household and are recorded in some surviving diaries.

There must have been great suspicion surrounding Her Majesty's interest in the paranormal. The Queen threatened that she was about to write a book about her paranormal experiences. When Randall Davidson, the then Dean of Windsor, later to become Archbishop of Canterbury, heard this he very nearly had apoplexy and threatened to resign saying that the Queen had gone too far. But Victoria was the last of the dictatorial monarchs - threats of resignations fell on deaf ears. The book was never written but not because of the Archbishop's or anyone else's threats. There must have been some very worried men in the hierarchy of both church and state in those days. On the old lady's death (Brown having died earlier) the order was given that every trace of

John Brown's influence to be erased from royal palaces. Statues, busts, and paintings of John Brown commissioned by the Queen, and that adorned the royal residences, were dismantled and destroyed. It was a purge reminiscent of the toppling of Lenin and Stalin statues in the immediate aftermath of the Berlin Wall's communist collapse. Church and State were determined that John Brown should become a '*non-person*'.

It seems amazing that almost fifty years after the Queen of England, Empress of half the world, had been defiantly holding seances with her gillie, that at the same time Helen Duncan, a truly remarkable medium was hauled before the courts and sentenced to nine months imprisonment for doing exactly the same thing.

Helen Duncan was a Scotswoman; her reputation as a medium had spread far and wide.

Her seances were always filled to the capacity she would allow. Suddenly, during one such séance, the police swooped. Helen was arrested. Charges against her were brought under the ancient *Witchcraft and Vagrancy Act*. This, unbelievably, was in 1944. She was charged with pretending to have powers of mediumship, and pretending she was able to contact the dead. Helen told His Lordships that it was no pretence, but that she was in fact a medium and she had in fact the powers to contact spirits from beyond the grave. She asked the court's permission to demonstrate her gifts. Permission was refused.

Helen Duncan was imprisoned for doing, publicly, exactly what many people knew her Queen had been doing privately fifty years before. She was imprisoned and made to promise never to hold another séance.

Years later, in 1956, Helen Duncan was staying at the home of friends in Nottingham. Contrary to her parole conditions she was persuaded to take part in a demonstration at a private séance. She sat at the table and entered into a deep trance. She was beginning to deliver her messages when the police again raided the house. It was obvious that her host had a whistle blower in his party. Two policemen rushed to take hold of her. Those present tried to warn them not to touch her; that touching a person in deep trace could cause a serious physical injury to the person. But the 'Old Bill' would have none of it. They grabbed her and pulled her to her feet. She collapsed in their arms and when the police failed to resuscitate her she was rushed to hospital by ambulance. She died three weeks later.

The post-mortem report stated that she had died of severe burns. And that these burns had been particularly severe in the region of her solar plexus; the area regarded by mediums as the body's main centre of ectoplasm. This incident brings home the words of the hymn about the different treatments meted out to rich and poor in days of yore:

"The rich man in his castle,
"The poor man at his gate."

There was another Royal story attributed this time to the coronation of King Edward VII. It was said that the King was very nearly killed on the day of his coronation. Edward VII apparently was a very superstitious person (as was his father, Prince Albert) - never thirteen at table, throw salt over the right shoulder – that sort of superstitious. But apparently it was not any of these taboos that saved his regal head. He was saved, so was recorded at the time, by a spirit guide who appeared to his gentleman-in-waiting; the Duke of Portland. The Duke, who was one of the chief organisers of Edward's coronation, had a vivid dream. He dreamt he could see the Royal open landau carriage being pulled at a fast cavalry trot through the archways of Horse Guards *en route* to Westminster Abbey ... and it crashed. The spirit guide dream - or vision - was so vivid that the old Duke ordered Colonel Ewart, the Crown Equerry, to go and measure the height and width of the Horse Guards archway, and carry out a general check. Ewart probably thought the Duke might have had a glass of port too many. "Monarchs have driven under that arch for generations," he would have blustered. But soldiers being soldiers he went with his measuring stick ... and measured.

"And what do you think of my dream then Ewart?" demanded the Duke once Ewart had returned to the palace.

"I think it's damned fortunate you had one, sir." replied the ashen-faced Colonel. The headroom was two feet too low!

The road had been raised 24 inches during innumerable repairs since the royal carriage had last been used, and the Coronation landau was taller than all the other royal carriages regularly using the Horse Guard route. Without a doubt the new king would have been decapitated if he had travelled in the royal coach on that particular route. It was a strange story told at the time, but one which is plausible.

Our late Elizabeth the Queen Mother certainly adds to the interest the Royal family had in the paranormal. She had been brought up in Glamis Castle, her family-seat castle in the Highlands of Scotland; a castle that was said to have been haunted by Lady Jane Grey, and the little Black Boy, and many, many other spirits of the past.

Elizabeth Bowes-Lyon, as she was then, was suspected of having had psychic powers even as a child. During the First World War the Queen Mother had already lost her eldest brother, Fergus, to Kaiser Bill. Within a short time news was brought to Glamis Castle that her other brother, Michael, had also been killed in action. Neither the young Elizabeth, nor her younger brother David, would accept the official posting of Michael's death. David refused to wear the regulation black mourning and the little Lady Elizabeth supported him.

They both said that they had seen spiritual images of Michael as, 'the ghost of a living man', a phenomena I describe in my earlier book, *"Holy Ghostbuster."* The children insisted that Michael was "… in a big house with fir trees all around it. He must be very ill," they had said, "because he's got a cloth tied around his head." David had also seen 'grey people', and had seen his brother Michael twice.

Everyone else was in deep bereavement. Shutters were drawn, black veils worn, a stately home in mourning. All that was missing was the corpse of a brave young officer called Lord Michael Bowes–Lyons. Three months later came confirmation that - as Elizabeth and David already knew - Michael was alive. But only just.

Badly wounded he certainly was; his head, as the children knew, heavily bandaged and he was resting in a field hospital surrounded exactly as they had described by ... fir trees.

As one would expect, members of the Royal Family like the rest of us have their own personal spirit guides. But it certainly appears that amongst royalty there seems to be a higher order of guidemanship. It seems as if there is a special Royal Corps of Spirit Guides whose work it is to preserve not just royal personages but the Monarchy itself. This special Royal Corps of Spirit Guides is called upon to take up duties at times when the Monarchy itself is at greatest risk.

We have a wonderful example of this in that period around the 1935's. It was the time when the life of King George V was drawing to its close that the Royal Guides were summoned to use every means they possessed to protect the very existence of the Monarchy.

The first human person chosen by the Royal Corps of Spirit Guides to help was a Mrs Margaret Moore. She was the wife of Dr. Gordon Moore who was a royal physician. Mrs Moore was a lady who possessed psychic powers and who was known amongst her friends as a person who attended seances. Her husband, as royal physician, was a person whom, one would have expected, had a way of contacting members of the royal family.

Mrs Margaret Moore reports that on a day in March 1935 she was unexpectedly invited to a select London private member's club; there to meet a high ranking Member of Parliament and his wife.

The distinguished politician told her: "We have been told by a mutual friend that you are a person who receives, and can understand, messages from the unseen." He went on to explain: "My wife is also a medium. She has received several messages of late that our majesty the King is about to die … fairly soon we fear. The guide that brought this message was anxious that it be passed on to the person who will succeed him. That person must be told so that he can prepare himself for the responsibly that is going to be thrust upon him." The Member of Parliament had then said; "We were wondering, madam, if you, or your husband, who has daily contact with members of the Royal Family, would undertake to do this."

Mrs Moore replied that she too had received messages to say that the King was dying.

But she told her MP friend; "Surely the Prince of Wales will succeed and he has been prepared and nurtured from childhood to succeed his father?" "_No_!" interrupted the MP, "the Prince of Wales will _not_ succeed; he will leave the country and a younger son will accede to the throne. This son has never been trained for kingship, nor does he know he is to be crowned in a very short time. It is he who should be warned of the great responsibility that is to befall him." If this account is to be believed it was obvious that the forthcoming abdication of Edward VIII and the coronation of his younger brother, George VI, were matters foreknown in the afterlife. The problem was that the guide spirit, who knew of the imminent death of the old king, did not seem to have direct access to the younger son, George, the Duke of York, who would succeed.

And it appears also that the attempts to conscript the help of Mrs Margaret Moore through the offices of a senior Member of Parliament and his wife also came to nought. She refused the commission to tell the King that he was dying or to warn his son, the Duke of York, to take a crash course in succession. She knew that, even if she failed in her mission, she would not be thrown into the Tower with an 'off with her head' proclamation. But she also knew that it could have been the means of bringing her husband's lucrative post as Physician to the Royal Household to a very premature end.

There must have been panic within the ranks of the Royal Corps of Spirit Guides when this happened. The Duke simply had to be warned. For them, the first scheme had failed; another had now to be put in motion.

The guide drama now moves to the old Empire country of Australia. Here there lived a happily married man, who had children, and a flourishing profession as a speech therapist. His name was Lionel Louge. Unexpectedly this man, Lionel Louge, had a sudden and inexplicable urge to sell his home, turn his back on his Australian business, and take his wife and children to a new life - in London, England. Amazingly he had only been in this country a few months before he found himself appointed as Speech Therapist to His Royal Highness the Duke of York.

It has to be explained at this point to younger generation readers what a very important office of state this was that had been suddenly thrust upon the speech therapist from Australia.

George, Duke of York, was married to Lady Elizabeth Bowes-Lyons, the late 'Queen Mum'; he was the father of Elizabeth, our present Queen, and Princess Margaret. George VI was a pathetically shy man and a hopeless stammerer and, as was found later, was appalled at the idea that he was to become king. He and his wife Elizabeth and their two children were greatly loved, but the poor Duke of York was the butt of cartoonists' humour and satire fodder to the columnists' pens; most of all because of his chronic stammer. However, Lionel Louge, the speech therapist from Melbourne, Australia, the man who had felt the urge to leave everything behind him and come, on a hunch, to London, made great strides at curing the Duke's awful stutter. So much so that George VI was able, on his first Christmas as King, to address his people throughout the world in a Radio Broadcast. I can well remember that broadcast when as a youth, and along with millions of others, I was almost willing the new king to find the next phrase. It was a great broadcast, and it was the birth of a king who was to lead his people safely through all the trails of a cruel and bitter Second World War.

It was also a first for the BBC in that it was the first-ever live Christmas radio broadcast from a monarch.

The king must have felt very grateful to his new-found teacher because there are reports of many visits that followed.

Lionel was not a 'kiss and tell' person but we have it on record how King George VI said to him during one of their informal get togethers: "My family, Lionel, are no strangers to spiritism. I suppose you have heard how Archbishop Randall Davidson and his secretary cleared away all the documents relating to my great grandmother's paranormal activities. Well I can tell you they didn't get their hands on *all* of them because we found some they failed to find – and I can assure you they are *very* interesting.'

Thereafter, Hannan Swaffer, that hard-nosed swaggering Fleet Street tabloid journalist of the 1940's and 50's and Lionel Louge became great friends. I have no idea whether Lionel was a spiritualist whilst he lived in Australia but Hannen Swaffer scoffed at the new religion of spiritualism. Yet strangely both men were soon to be converted to the newly formed Spiritualist Church.

Hannen Swaffer, it is reported, arranged a sitting for Lionel with Mrs. Lillian Bailey, the leading medium of the day. Neither had met previously. That's a matter of fact. And Mrs Bailey had no knowledge of Lionel's connections with the Royal family. Hannen Swaffer reports that at that meeting (a séance of types) with Lionel, Mrs Bailey delivered a message to him. She said: "There is a gentleman here who wishes me to thank you for everything you did for his son." Lionel, not wishing to give away the identity of the 'gentleman with a message', merely replied "I quite understand, sir." He was addressing the late King; George VI's father.

One must ask why so many of the Establishment spirit guides became so involved in this business of preparing King George VI for office and particularly for ridding him of his stammer. He, after all, was just another in a long line of monarchs. Some cruel and murderous, some crippled and mentally handicapped, and others just simply mad. Stuttering seems to be the least of royal lineage problems.

One can only assume that the guides responsible for the protection of Institutions and the preservation of Nations felt that this time democracy itself was at risk. They were protecting not just members of the Royal family. They, with their foreknowledge, would know that this un-trained, un-prepared, abysmally shy, stuttering person would be the one that would have to lead his country through World War II. This scourge which came upon us in 1939 was no ordinary war. It was a war, which would have had the most calamitous implications if things went wrong.

George VI was the '*Weakest Link*'. Big brother, the abdicated Edward, Prince of Wales, would have been even weaker.

All these tales of the Royal Family's dabbling with the paranormal and holding seances to contact the departed might seem strange. But the strangest thing of all was finding that at the time Queen Victoria and John Brown were sitting together in séance, and very nearly up to the time our present Queen was enthroned, the *Witchcraft Act* of 1735 still remained on the statute book. Parliament spent the whole of the first day of December 1950 debating the repeal of the Witchcraft Act, which – over centuries - had condemned so many women, many of them wise and intelligent women, to violent and cruel death as witches.

It frightens me to think that in 1950, before the act was repealed, I was very much in demand by people whose houses were haunted by ghosts, but I was never arrested for it. I was not even threatened with arrest. Some might say "Ah yes, there are so many of these antiquated laws on our statute books but they have become obsolete over the years." But the Nottingham Police certainly did not regard this ancient Act obsolete in the case of Helen Duncan.

She was arrested in 1944 and charged under the *Witchcraft Act* of pretending she was a medium who could make contact with the dead. She was imprisoned.

Eight years later, at a time when I had been the Vicar of Llandegai for four years, she was re-arrested and as a result of being manhandled by police whilst in deep trance died within weeks. To find that all this could have been going on in this country as recently as half a century ago is truly amazing. I can't even understand how I came to miss out on it.

I found later that Hannen Swaffer, the convert to Spiritualism, had castigated the government in his regular column in the *Sunday People* for its great injustice.

It was a great read. It stirred up public feeling. Air Vice Marshal Dowding and Hannen Swaffer, both by now adherents of the new Spiritualist Church, and Maurice Brabanell, editor of the *Psychic News* activated the Press.

Helen Duncan became the first martyr of the Spiritualist teaching.

After her death, and after the resulting repeal of the *Witchcraft Act*, others could now openly speak of their visions and the appearances from the beyond that they had experienced.

Artist Ifor James's portrait of Ham Hoi, one of Elwyn's spirit guides.
(See Chapter: "My Guide")

And Elwyn's other spirit guide, an 18th century priest.

Ziggy Bossowski, 81, being routinely breathalysed by Major Bob Card before undertaking a remarkable parachute sky-dive over Holland in 1994. (See: Guides Under Stress)

The Team: author Aelwyn Roberts, (left)
and 'sensitive', Elwyn Roberts

Chapter Six
HOW IT'S DONE

Now at this stage, please allow me to deviate as a sort of preamble to the chapter "*How It's Done.*" Let me for a few moments take off my parapsychology hat and put on my clergyman's hat.

When a person lies dying in hospital or at home and his heart, brain and vital organs are rapidly 'shutting down', he is, at this point, passing through the most exciting and the most pleasurably anguishing experience since being born.

He may have lived through the terrors of war or confronted other traumas in life, but these experiences are nothing to be compared with the experience of his passing over. His earth body is being removed and with it all those little pains that he had got used to over many years. He has to vest himself in his new spirit body with its lightness and its litheness.

Using this body, he has now to travel through the tunnel of light and joy and beautiful music. He can see in the distance family and friends who have gone before him but who are there now standing at the fence waving to him – welcoming him. But not before he has been greeted by the White Light which fills the air around with an aura of joy, peace and love.

We know all this because thousands of people who had technically died, but who have been resuscitated in hospitals all over the world have told us so. Their stories are so vivid and constant in almost every detail. We also know it because it has been written in the Tibetan Book of the Dead documented centuries ago.

Whilst the still figure on the bed upstairs is experiencing its hour of ecstasy, the family downstairs are planning a time roster for those who will keep deathbed vigils. Children and grandchildren cannot bear the thought of old granddad dying a lonely death. Someone has to be there with him. They don't quite know why because the old man has been in a comma for the last two days.

The two sons will perhaps take over the first vigil. They talk together across the bed to break the errieness. They talk about the things they know about – their work and their ambitions and sometimes they talk about football and about the weekly pub-quiz in the 'Black Bull'. After all, they say, poor old dad is unconscious; he can't hear a word.

But they are wrong. Medical science tells us that the last faculty to leave the body is the faculty of hearing. The talk of Manchester United's victory over Leeds FC is probably an irritating distraction to a dying man during his greatest hour. He's probably screaming at them mentally: "For the love of Pete! Shut up lads and give me peace to get on with my job of passing over."

I know when my time comes, I would love to have one of my loved ones by my bed. And I'd like the 'duty' vigil to identify himself or herself. "Hi Taid, this is Emma or Tom or whoever." But then, after holding my hand for a moment or two, to then sit quietly and get on with their reading, or crossword and give me space to get on with the most exciting thing that will have happened to me … my crossing over.

That deviation was, I hope, worth it. The issue is so important. I'll now lay down my clergyman's hat and reach again for my 'parasycholgist's' cap and continue …

Those who have read my other books on the paranormal will know how the team works, and will have a rough idea of the kind of ghosts we work with. Past readers will have to bear with me. It is essential that new readers be brought into the picture before we tackle the big bullyboys of the spirit world, or to be fair, the group that produces some of the biggest bullyboys of the spirit world ... the poltergeists.

Ordinary spirits, or ghosts, are fairly easy to understand and easy to get on with. They are 'yesterday's people', some of whom have left this world many years ago; others who left so recently that we would have known them in their earth life.

They are also fairly easy to understand because they still use the same minds they used on earth; human minds. They also seem to retain their own native language. But they now live in a different environment and this does create some amount of difficulty.

For example ghosts have little knowledge of currency. Money whether pounds, shillings, and pence, or decimal, is a topic which has become vague and fuzzy to them. The 'euro' would be a definite taboo! They get confused if money enters into the conversation. Similarly dates will confuse them.

Ask them "When did you live on earth?" or "When did you die?" and you add to their confusion, so much so that many will cease to answer and others will simply shuffle off.

We on earth are governed by the idea of time in the three stages of past, present, and future. We passed an exam two years ago (in the past); we intend to retire in four years time (in the future); we are having lunch today (present). Spirits seem to live in a timeless state, or in the "eternal present." "In four years time," means as little to them as the fact that we passed our exam two years ago. Their behaviour, I find, is similar to that of people who have emigrated to another country. In their new country they have their own currency, their own traditions and their own system of measuring time. The ways of the old country soon begin to fade.

But memories both personal and of families left behind still remain crystal clear. It surprises me at times the detail contained in messages given from the beyond to a husband or a wife on this side. Very often the clue is given in recollection of a most insignificant happening that only the two of them would know about or even bother to remember. "Tell him it is a message from the person whose chair broke when he laughed at our anniversary supper," will come a message from beyond. And someone will. Vividly.

And it is because their memories of life on earth are so lucid that they regard it as such a great treat to be able to return from time to time to see the old home where they lived, or their old golf-club, or where they got married, or, as sometimes, the room where they gave birth to their first child.

I sometimes think we've got it all wrong when we carry arms full of flowers to place on the graves of dear ones to commemorate their birthdays, or to let them know that we are still thinking of them at the graveside at Christmas or on Mother's Day. I have come to believe that a churchyard or a cemetery is about the last place a spirit, given the chance of an earth visit, would want to see. Churchyards are 'no-go' areas for ghosts. I have the feeling that it would be a much wiser way of remembering the birthdays of our dear ones if we placed the flowers in a vase on our living room table.

I would say that I have met three different types of ghosts. In the first category are those I would call the busy-body ghosts. Somehow they have found a way of crossing back and forth from the hereafter to earth. They enjoy coming back just to see how things are getting along in the old home or school or workplace, but not as I have said, the churchyard or the cemetery where they were buried.

The second group comprise those who have crossed over, and once having arrived at the other side realise they still have some weighty matters pressing on their consciences and, because of this, are unable to settle down in the spirit world. On one occasion Elwyn and I were invited to help a young mother of three children. She was suffering from the most horrible depression which neither therapy nor drugs could remove. We found after we called that she was also suffering the monotony of a nightly visit from the ghost of her husband. He had committed suicide. Night after night he would visit and sit on her bed saying nothing. She, poor girl, complained that whilst this happened she was neither married nor widowed and that someone should tell him he was dead and that he should leave her and her little family alone. Elwyn's therapy worked. With the young mother's permission he placed her in a state of light hypnotism. Through his gift of mediumship he was able to let the wife and her dead husband talk to each other. The dead husband told her that he was coming every night hoping to be able to tell her how sorry he was for his suicide, to explain that he knew how selfish he had been leaving her alone to cope with the children. He wanted her to know that he still loved her. Could she forgive him for what he had done? I could only hear her side of the conversation, she said: "Of course I forgive you darling. And when we were together I loved you more than anything in the world. But you are dead now," she added, "and you must leave us."

At the end of the little meeting tears streamed down the young mother's cheeks but she had a happy smile on her face. She knew her troubles were over and that she could return her *Vallium* and *Prozac* tablets to the surgery as no longer necessary.

The third type of ghost I have encountered are earthbound ghosts. These are they that have died and yet somehow don't realise they are dead. They've gone to the banks of the Jordan and have for some unknown reason failed to find the crossing place. They've come back to their own home, or place of work, where they try to carry on their life as before. I know this is an awful thought and so I hasten to add that earth bound ghosts are exceptionally rare. It is the main task of the Spiritualist Church to rescue such people and set them on the right track. There are also, we are told, a great number of spirit guides on the other side who form Rescue Squads to aid the earth bound. These guides are very highly trained for this work and exceedingly efficient.

Ghosts that I know next to nothing about, and have never met to the best of my knowledge, are the Anniversary Ghosts.

These are the ghosts that seem to manifest themselves on earth on the anniversary of their death or the commemoration of something traumatic that happened to them in their lives. Once a year they seem to return to earth to re-enact this agonising experience they suffered in life. There is the often quoted experience of poor Ann Boleyn who once every year, "walks the bloody tower with the head tucked underneath her arm." There is also a room in a certain college in Oxford where a student suicide is regularly re-enacted once a year. There are also many tales of people hearing noises from the sites of wartime RAF stations. The old RAF station at Bircham Newton, Norfolk, is famous for them as any of hundreds of thousands of construction industry workers who have trained there since it became home of the CITB will know. The two WWII aviators who 'haunt' the Bircham Newton squash courts have sent otherwise hardened builders gibbering back to their quarters. Elsewhere witnesses to anniversary ghosts will describe the noise; "it was as if the RAF airfield of the 1940's had come alive again. I could hear the voices of men shouting and of planes taking off into the sky." Again, Bircham Newton has its 'phantom' aircraft heard by hundreds of people on particular calendar days to be taking off into some timeless WWII re-enaction.

But as I say these are things beyond my ken.

So now, before we move on to the next chapters, I would like to introduce you to the most enigmatic of all spirits - the Poltergeist.

Poltergeists are different from other ghosts; they are very, very different. So much so that there are a growing number of para-psychologists that say that a poltergeist is not a spirit at all.   Poltergeist activity, they insist, has nothing whatsoever to do with the spirits of the departed. Poltergeists, according to them, are all man-made.   They maintain that all the activity attributed to a poltergeist is created by a power or energy emanating from the human mind.   They would have us believe that the loud noises and the stone throwing, the lifting of massive weights and the often wanton destruction carried out by them is all done unknowingly, unwittingly by a human mind that misfires and becomes able to generate a power they call psycho-kinetic power.   The same people tell us that the best mind material for producing this kinetic energy is the mind of a child.   Or the minds of two or more children co-acting or in contradiction to each other.   This phenomenon, they say, can perform Herculean tasks.   This is why at the beginning of most inquires into poltergeist inquires the investigator's first question is, "Are there any children living in this house?"

I don't agree with these people.   I don't even pretend to understand their argument.   I believe poltergeists are originally spirits or ghosts; possibly earthbound spirits. They are spirits or ghosts who have discovered that all humans carry within themselves some kind of ethereal salve. In some humans this juice or salve overflows.   Spirits, by imbibing it, retain all the benefits of having a spirit body (they can walk through walls, travel at speed, be in several places at the same time) but they also re-acquire some of the old human benefits (of lifting weights, throwing objects, and even talking).   In a sense poltergeists are hybrid beings; part spirit, part human. They retain the human part of their make up by feeding on the ethereal salve from their human suppliers. They are, in effect, vampire spirits. They exist - at least as poltergeists - for as long as they are able to draw their sustenance from their human victims. But like the kinetic-power school, I would still ask the initial question if asked to investigate poltergeist activity: "Are there children in the house?" But I'd ask it for a very different reason. Children seem to overflow the ethereal salve more that adults. They form the most common focal attraction for poltergeists.

I am not alone in thinking this. Readers will find that Professor David Fontana in his report on the case of 'Pete' of Cardiff is able to name the person who supplied 'Pete' with his energy. I quote:

> "Paul seems in fact to have been the major focus of the activities. This is consistent with similar cases where one individual usually seems to supply the physical energy upon which the poltergeist is said to draw."

In the case of the Enfield Poltergeist which you'll come to read about, Dodo the medium who eventually sent him packing, was reputed to have had said, "First I will have to cure the people in the house." He explained that these were the people with leaking 'energy containers'. Stop the leakage, he said, and starve the poltergeist.

So there we are. A poltergeist according to some is created by a kind of an explosion in the human mind that releases kinetic energy which in turn produces the poltergeist effect.

Others believe a poltergeist is a ghost who has found the means of imbibing into himself 'juices' from the human person that enables it to perform human acts such as throwing and moving objects and even talking. The title poltergeist is German. It means *polter* (loud) *geist* (ghost).

Some poltergeists can be evil and nasty, selfish and destructive. But only a few. Poltergeists, like football fans, are very often miss-represented. Imagine 40,000 fans wending their way to a football match on a Saturday afternoon. Forty of them will stay behind to fight after the game, cutting each other with blades and broken bottles. These few are called football hooligans. The following morning it is the thuggish behaviour of the 40 football hooligans which is reported in the Sunday press. There is no mention of the other 39,960 who went happily home for their tea. Similarly it is only the behaviour of the horrible Enfield type poltergeists which is chronicled in books and reported in newspapers. 'Pete' of Cardiff and Harold of Bala didn't hurt anyone. They were just being a little mischievous. I know of a ladies' hairdressing salon not far from my home that has its own poltergeist; a poltergeist that is practically a member of the staff. He performs all kinds of little tricks whilst the ladies sit in their chairs waiting for the perm to set. A pair of scissors is thrown into the air at speed and then made to drop gently on the table in front of the customer. Harmless stuff with '*no malice aforethought*'. The nasty poltergeists are the small number of ghost hooligans who manage to get books written about them and who grab the newspaper headlines.

So that is the cast we work with in this drama. Now it is necessary for you to meet the camera crew if I may be allowed to mix my metaphors.

Elwyn Roberts and I, Aelwyn Roberts, work as a team. We have worked together and trampled through a vast number of haunted houses for many, many years; forty or more I would say. I am a clergyman, priested nearly 60 years ago. When I was a young curate in the early 1950's I was challenged by elders of a Spiritualist Church to attend one of their séances in their meeting rooms. My old friend the late Ifan O.Williams was a producer of features programmes on BBC Radio Wales. He warned me not go near their place. "They will have it all wired up and they will frighten the pants off you," he said. "Leave it to me and I'll fix this contest on neutral ground."

Within days he was back on the phone. "I have found the most haunted house in Wales," he said triumphantly, "and using BBC research cash, I have engaged the two best mediums in the country. We're going there next Friday evening." He was inviting a BBC co-producer to come along and also the late Emrys Williams the BBC's top sound-engineer at the time. Also invited were prominent members of the Society for Psychical Research. It was left to me to invite my Spiritualist Church elders. He was telling no one where the house was. We were to meet at seven o'clock outside Rhyl railway station where he would pick up the two mediums then we'd travel in convoy to the 'Most Haunted House' in Wales.

On this particular night great and wonderful things happened. In this house we met an earthbound spirit locally called '*I'm Coming*'.[1] 'I'm Coming' had apparently been dead for 30 years. It was the first ghost I had ever seen in my life. 'I'm Coming' was a monoglot Welshman. As a fellow countryman of his, the English mediums asked me to speak to him and to interpret to them what he was saying.

That night I received my baptism-by-fire into the paranormal world. This night, arranged by Ifan.O Williams was a night to remember! It was a night I would recount many years later in my very first book on the paranormal 'Holy Ghostbuster'. The day following our visit the *Liverpool Daily Post* newspaper ran a front page story headlined: 'FOUR BANGOR MEN IN HAUNTED HOUSE'. That blaze of publicity opened the floodgates.

We found that there were in North Wales in the early 1950's a huge number of people who were troubled by ghosts. They were not just curious to know about ghosts but terrified by the presence of ghosts in their homes. Many were contemplating changing house to be rid of their tormentors; others so terrified of the dark that their health was suffering. There were some that had not dared go upstairs at night, in their own homes, for many years and they

---

[1] "*I'm Coming*" derived his name from his earthly – and ghost-life – occupation as a publican. As a 'living' landlord he'd spend much of his day in the pub cellar, listening out for footsteps of his regulars in the bar above. "I'm coming!" he'd shout as he heard them tap for replenishment. It was a habit he failed to shake off when he returned to the pub in afterlife; still haunting the old staircase between cellar and bar. "*I'm coming*" was his ghostly hallmark.

all felt quite unable to tell of their fears even to family or friends for fear of ridicule.

Many read the story of the 'Four Bangor Men in a Haunted House' on the front page of the *Daily Post*. They noted the fact that one of the four was a clergyman, the Reverend Aelwyn Roberts. Surely, they argued, a clergyman who visited a haunted house and who spoke to ghosts would never ridicule their story. And even if unable to help, a clergyman was a person who would keep a confidence. He certainly wouldn't laugh at them.

My telephone didn't stop ringing.

But unfortunately the clergyman in question was not, is not and probably never shall be a medium or a sensitive. He has not an iota of psychic power. I had no idea then how to deal with the problems of these people, apart from giving them the comfort of a sympathetic listening, and praying with them.

Months later having travelled home from preaching a harvest-festival service in Anglesey I sat down and listened to a most fascinating programme on BBC Radio Wales. A young man called Elwyn Roberts had, apparently, hypnotised a young woman and was getting her to regress to the age of six. She was telling him - in the voice of a very young child - how she sang and won a prize in their local eisteddfod. He was asking her if she still remembered what she had sung, and could she sing it now? Out came the children's favourite Welsh song;

"M' welais Jack-y-Do, yn eistedd ar y to;

Het wen ar ei ben a dwy goes bren,
Ho ho, ho ho, ho ho!"

And all in the breathy-voice of a six-year-old. That night I made up my mind that I would have to meet this young man Elwyn Roberts.

Elwyn doesn't like being referred to as a medium. He tells me that a medium is someone associated with the Spiritualist Church, or who officiates in Spiritualist churches, and he is *not* a spiritualist. He describes himself rather as a sensitive. I would add that in this case he must be the most sensitive-sensitive, that I have ever met; and I have met a good few since my time in Ifan O's haunted house of fifty years ago. Furthermore, Elwyn is one of those rare sensitives that one describes as a trans-medium, or a trans-sensitive.

His psychic power is such that he enables the spirits to manifest themselves into him and also, at the same time, to duffers like me so that I, too, can see and talk to them.

So when later calls for help came the Elwyn-Aelwyn duo would respond and offer practical help. We made a good team.

The moment Elwyn arrives at a house he sees, or feels, or hears a presence from the beyond. But he says nothing; at least not until we have had our little relaxation get-together.

I remember on one occasion Elwyn and I were driving on our way to a house in Anglesey reputed to have been occupied by a horrible monster of a woman ghost. In the back seat of the car was the human tenant of the house, a young man, who had been so terrified by the ghost a few nights before Christmas, that he had run half a mile clad only in his pyjamas to seek refuge. That night, he had sworn that he would never ever again return to this horrible house. This evening he was sitting on the back seat dying to tell Elwyn of his experiences, but warned by me, on pain of death, not to. Elwyn never wants to hear what has been going on in a house. It confuses him; it's like throwing up a smokescreen. On this particular evening we were drawing into a garage for petrol. We were a good eight miles from the ghost-house when Elwyn suddenly said: "I think I can see your lady ghost. She is short, she has two rosy cheeks; the face and complexion of a person who lives an outdoor life. And she is wearing a massive apron made of sacking."

"That's her! That's the one!" squeaked the excited voice from the backseat.

"And I also have a name for her," continued Elwyn. "Her name is Hannah."

When we arrived at the house Hannah was there to greet us. She wanted to talk, she was pleased to have company, and she looked nothing like the monster ghost that our host had described to me. That night I was able to chat to Hannah about Lloyd George and she also described to me the difficulty of farming during the First World War. I asked Hannah where she had been buried. The following day, following her instructions, I stood by her grave with its head stone inscribed with her name on it. I describe Hannah in my book 'Holy Ghostbuster' as the Extrovert Ghost.

Elwyn and I have carried on in this way for many years. Elwyn finding the errant spirits and enabling them to manifest themselves and talk to me, the clergyman; I questioning and counselling them. (It is quite amazing how many of us take little problems and worries and matters of often trivial conscience with us to the grave).

Then one day came a call from another Elwyn. He was Elwyn Edwards, a poet, living in Bala. He had a problem. He was converting an old house he had bought into flats. But when the work was nearing completion the workmen walked out - or rather ran out. They said they had met a ghost there and that the horrible smell this ghost had given off had caused them to cough, and their eyes to smart. Elwyn Edwards told me; "It's this awful stench in the house that's worrying me. The men are right. I have smelt it myself many times. It's a wonder to me the workmen have put up with it for so long. If something isn't done about the stink no one will rent my flats." He had a point. The stench was abominable.

I promised Mr Edwards I would help but that I would have to bring Elwyn Roberts with me. When I said this, Elwyn Edwards, the local poet, stood agog. I thought he was going to bow or genuflect as he uttered the name. "Elwyn Roberts?" He repeated it, "Do you mean Elwyn Roberts the Chief Bard?" I had quite forgotten that my friend Elwyn Roberts had been declared a Crowned Bard of Wales at the National Eisteddfod the previous year. A visit from Elwyn Roberts, the Crown Bard, to Elwyn Edwards, the local poet, would be akin to a visit from Michael Jackson to a local teenybopper. For Elwyn Edwards, the local bard, our visit was to be a double whammy.

That night we discovered that our new friend was himself endowed with a fair amount of psychic power and that, more importantly perhaps, he was a meticulous researcher. Every date, every name, and every crumb of information given by a spirit during an evening visit would be thoroughly researched the next day by our new-found partner in Bala.

Strangely, or perhaps not so strangely, within a few years of our meeting Elwyn Edwards, the local bard from Bala, was himself declared a Chaired Bard of the National Eisteddfod of Wales. I often teasingly remind the two of them that I should be the next one to receive poetic stimuli from our poet guides!

If any reader should visit Wales and see two Chief Bards of Wales accompanied by a white haired old clergyman walking across a village square you will know that there is probably a ghost somewhere in close proximity!

When the team arrives at a house to do a particular job we sit down with the family as any other visitors would. We accept the kind offer of cups of tea, we talk about all sorts of things - apart from ghosts that is - just to get a relaxed atmosphere in an otherwise tense situation.

Then, when the time is opportune, Elwyn will describe to us what he had probably seen the moment he entered the house; "I see a young woman," he will say, "She is standing by the door feeling a bit shy perhaps; wondering who the strangers are." This will be his commentary to us; to put us at ease. Then he'll addresses the young lady herself; "Come along my dear, do join us, don't be afraid. We are only here to help you."

Then once again he'll turn to us seated around; "She's coming up behind me. If you look towards my left shoulder you may be able to see her. She is about twenty years …"

He is often interrupted as this point by a gasp from several members of the family and a quiet whisper, *"Oh, I can see her!"*

And finally I, the non-psychic, will also see her - energised by Elwyn's surplus energy.

Elwyn then says something which always gives me the creeps. He always uses the same formula: "You may use my body if you know how." It's that "if you know how" that always gets me. I frequently worry to myself, what if they do know how to enter … and then find that they can't get out again! The spirit voice comes from Elwyn. It sometimes comes from his mouth but the resonance and tone can be sometimes different to his normal voice. It could be the soprano voice of a woman, or the voice of a child, or the deep voice of a man. Accents and language can change also. They're the voices of a spirit or spirits who will have accepted Elwyn's invitation to take over his body. They will also have presumed to borrow his voice box, and his vocal chords. But in most instances it is Elwyn's own human voice that we hear. Elwyn converses with the ghost in mind language. He then interprets to us what is being said: "She is saying to me that her father's name is William and that he is a tailor by trade."

I know it all sound so impossible, and so unreal when one comes to write it down.

We have never cluttered ourselves with equipment, cameras, tape recorders and the like but latterly we have acquired one piece of electrical aid. It is a little tablelamp with a small wattage red bulb and a small shade that throws the light on to Elwyn's face. I find this little lamp a great help. It is much easier now to see Elwyn's facial changes. When he says, "Use my body if you know how," the rest of us will know within seconds whether the invitation is being accepted or not. When his invitation is accepted his physical body changes. He begins to look younger, or older, depending on the age of the spirit that takes over. I have even seen clean-shaven Elwyn sprouting a very heavy black moustache. I thought at the time that it rather suited him.

I have to say all this so that the reader understands our trade-protocols.

When I say, "The spirit said that he was 25 years of age" it is rather that Elwyn says it, either in his own natural voice or in the spirit voice emanating through his vocal chords. And when I say, "We all saw the ghost smiling at this remark," it Elwyn's physical lips that are smiling, but at the behest of the spirit who has borrowed his facial muscles and nerves for this purpose.

I just can't understand why anyone should be afraid of ghosts.

Chapter Seven

MY POLTERGEIST HAROLD

Ghosts are so ordinary that if they do happen to hit the newspaper headlines they tend only to appear in the local press. A few extrovert poltergeists, however, have become so infamous they have `often made banner headlines in the national and international media.

One of the most horrible of these was one whom the world newspapers named the 'Bell Witch'. He invaded a peaceful farmhouse in Tennessee, USA, two hundred years ago and his horrible exploits are still talked about to this day.

John and Lucy Bell had nine children. They all lived happily on this farm in Tennessee in the early 1800's. That was until _he_ arrived.

It started off with the usual poltergeist activity; scraping of furniture, bedclothes pulled off the beds, stones thrown at the family and at the house from the outside. The focal point was one of the children called Elizabeth. She had her hair pulled and was slapped across the face so hard that observers noticed her cheeks reddening. Elizabeth's father became ill from some fever that was attributed to the poltergeist. He was unable to eat and his tongue became swollen. The poltergeist, which by this time had developed a voice, haunted him and said that he would be tormented like this to the end of his life. It was to become worse. As John Bell lay dying his bedclothes were dragged off his bed. The voice was heard swearing at him and rejoicing at his death and his suffering. After his death the poltergeist activity began to fade.

That was 1817... a long time ago. There have been suggestions that John Bell had been abusing his daughter, Elizabeth, and that she had managed to use polteristic energy, quite unbeknown to herself, to revenge herself on him. Following the long persecution the family were set free to live a normal life once again.

The 'Bell Witch' was, indeed, a bad poltergeist. There are others who also seem to possess this same superhuman strength and energy but who seem to keep themselves to themselves, doing their own thing and hurting no one. There was one of these poltergeists that lived in an old mansion house in Anglesey. His one great joy was to be able to welcome a new baby into the house in his own special way. The night of the baby's birth the family could expect the furniture within the house's vast library to be pushed to the middle of the room. It was done very quietly and methodically. The heavy mahogany desk and chairs together with all the tall mahogany bookshelves, laden with their tons of leather-bound books, were all pushed into the centre of the room. Then, in some inexplicable way, the carpet was retrieved from under the weight of furniture and carefully rolled and placed on top. It was a job that ten men would have found difficult to perform in days. In poltergeist hands it was done at night without waking a single member of the family.

I asked a solicitor friend who had been born in the house, and whose birth had been celebrated by the moving of the library furniture, how his parents got the room right afterwards. He explained that the polteristic celebration lasted for about three days. One the third night after the birth all would be restored to its rightful place, sitting back snugly on it's carpet. His parents had enquired of previous tenants and they had advised them to simply do nothing. Restoration, they were told, would be quiet and would occur on the third or fourth night after the birth. I asked him if the operation was intended as a celebration of the birth of a child, or was it a protest that another noisy child had been born into the family home. Apparently no one knew, but it had been assumed since the whole process was carried out in such a quiet and stately manner, that it had a celebratory intention. Those who have studied the carryings on of poltergeists will say that their life span is no more that two to four years at the most. Towards the end of this period their strength diminishes and their voice becomes hoarse – they seem to fade back into the oblivion from whence they came. I have to admit that the industrious furniture-pushing old chap in Anglesey seems to be the exception. He is known to have performed his baby rights in the same house for many generations.

It is all these variants in behaviour, from the committing of murder, (some would say), to the innocent, childish, trick of hiding a handbag that makes it so difficult for anyone to define a poltergeist. But in this case, I think I can venture where others fear to tread. I have actually met, and spoken to a self-confessed poltergeist. He was even kind enough to tell my friends and me why he had behaved so abominably.

My psychic friends and I caught him in the house of Rhodri and Meiriona in Bala, North Wales. We talked to him. He told us why he hated his victim and why he took such pleasure persecuting him. Eventually we helped our friend, the poltergeist, find his way to the *Summerland* where he belonged.

Rhodri and Meiriona have five children. Delyth, Anita, Lucia, Meirion and Anest. Rhodri is a mountain sheep farmer. Meiriona has a job as a receptionist. Their house is packed from cellar to attic with ghosts from practically any generation you can think of; but you couldn't wish to see a happier human family on God's earth than the one who is co-tenanting with these ghosts.

Meiriona vibrates a psychic aura, perhaps not surprisingly, because her mother hailed from Latin South America. A great deal of Meiriona's sensitiveness has also rubbed off on her poet-farmer husband, Rhodri. This little family has no use for television. In the evenings you would probably find Meiriona and Rhodri experimenting with automatic writing, whilst the children are upstairs playing with their *"Beautiful Children"* friends. Delyth and Anita had been saying for some time that the beautiful children visit them and come and play in their bedroom at night. This was at first regarded as normal child romanticising. They said that the beautiful children would come to their bedroom in the evening and that they would have little concerts where the human children would sing and dance and recite, and the beautiful children would laugh and clap. Then the beautiful children would perform their tricks to the applause of the human children. One of the spirit children, apparently, would climb on top of the wardrobe and shout "bonjolaba! bonjolaba!" and they would all laugh. Delyth tells us that on one occasion when they were all discussing how light the spirit children were she got out their bathroom scales to weigh them. One of them only weighed one ounce but most of them came up to three-ounce mark.

But the beautiful children are no longer thought of as child imaginings or fantasies in this household. When some of my friends were present at the house one evening, one of the beautiful children appeared in the room with them. Delyth said that his name was Joshua, and that he was one of those who came to play in their room. As they were looking at him he popped into an old photo of their grandmother. Their mother, Meiriona, said she too could still see him and she described him to the others. "He is an Indian," she said. "He has long jet black hair and he is going in and out of the photograph on the wall." Then Rhodri was able to see him as well. My friend Elwyn Edwards asked Meiriona if he was a Red Indian. "No," she replied "he is a little boy from India. He is about ten years of age." This went on for about ten minutes with the children and the parents describing to the rest of those present all that went on. Then the antics of Joshua grew fainter and he disappeared.

One can well understand how this kind of a home also became a home from home for many of us who take an interest in things paranormal and particularly in the living habits of ghosts. If anyone were to offer me a £100 for showing him a "real ghost" that he could see and hear it would be to this house in Bala that I would travel. The odds are good that I would be £100 in pocket by the end of the day. This little family co-habit with ghosts, and ghosts integrate with them. I told Rhodri that I was going to try and write a book about poltergeists and that I was even going to try and define this thing that caused such an upheaval in people's homes. Rhodri innocently asked me, "Don't people know what poltergeists are then?" I told him that I hadn't come across a satisfactory answer yet. "It's a pity people don't know," he said. "Before you write your next book why don't come over to the house and we'll ask the old man, old Gwilym Mercia, what a poltergeist is. He's a knowledgeable old man. He'll tell you." Rhodri was referring to his Guardian Spirit.

One night when we were all at the house, Rhodri told Elwyn Roberts that he would love to meet his guardian spirit. So Elwyn passed on the message to the void; "Rhodri would dearly love to meet his guardian spirit." In no time at all there was a stirring and we could see sitting in Elwyn's chair this rather obese, totally hairless, old man. He just sat there saying nothing apart from telling us that his name was Gwilym Mercia. Then he simply disappeared. After this he would turn up quite regularly at our little sessions. Elwyn Edwards - his near neighbour in Bala - seemed to have the knack of extracting a little more information from Gwilym Mercia than rest of us. He also began a most complicated research study in archives and college libraries to try and find more about this man who wore ancient clothes and called himself *Gwilym Mercia.* Elwyn Edwards is a wonderful researcher. After months he told us that he was pretty sure he knew the identity of Rhodri's guide. He was, he told us "William of March" (the guide had given us the Welsh version of his name, Gwilym Mercia) and he had been Bishop of Bath and Wells. Consecrated AD 1293; Died AD 1302. He had been Keeper of the Great Seal of England and a great favourite of King Edward I.

To enjoy Rhodri and Meiriona's home you have to flop into a chair, relax, and half close your eyes. There is no joy in this house for the edgy, the agitated, the apprehensive or the hyperactive. Rhodri should have a notice over his front door, "Only he who is relaxed, composed, serene and at peace with himself shall enter herein." And yet it was in this house that my friends and I caught our first elusive poltergeist.

For all the peace in Rhodri's house, there was one room to which no one would enter; at least no one entered to stay for any length of time! We all knew it as the 'cold room'. Even in summer it gave one the shivers. Rhodri was telling us how heavy furniture was being pushed into the middle of the room and moved back again days later. And he told us how his belongings were always going missing. He was a "roll your own" cigarette smoker. Very often when he knew he had left his tobacco pouch on the arm of a chair it would disappear for days only to reappear in some other part of the house later. Rhodri was always asking the children about these "carryings on."

The rest of us had come to the conclusion that amongst his other ghostly lodgers Rhodri was also harbouring a poltergeist. We knew too, the mayhem some poltergeists could create in a happy home if antagonised. It was all right for us; we could drive away from it at the end of the evening. Rhodri and his lovely little family would have to live with it possibly for years. So we did nothing.

I have no idea how it came about but after some months of this kind of goings-on Rhodri and Meiriona decided to give us the go ahead. They asked us to find out more about the tenant of the cold room.

On a certain night we left the comfort of the open fire in the lounge, we put on our overcoats, scarves and gloves, and proceeded into the cold middle room to sit on its upright farmhouse chairs around its heavy oak table. I knew Elwyn was afraid. He was the man who normally said when he felt the presence of a ghost. "Come along in. We are your friends. We are here to help you. Enter into my body if you know how too." This time Elwyn told me "I'm *not* going to let this fellow take over. He's a nasty one "

Elwyn sat behind his little red light. We could all see his face quite clearly. I think it is true to say that although we were all ghost-hardened we were all feeling a bit nervous on this occasion. We knew this one was not an ordinary run-of-the-mill kind of ghost. We didn't have long to wait. Normally Elwyn gives us some kind of pre-warning. This time he said nothing. There was no need. His face slowly changed into a glowering angry face. It was Elwyn sitting on that chair but the face was the face of the devil himself. Then suddenly the strangest thing happened. Rhodri shot out of his chair walked up to the grotesque face and bellowed at him: "Yes it's you, you bugger. I know you. I've seen you before. You are the bastard that pinches my cigarettes and hides my tools, and moves the bloody furniture around in the night." The face made a glowering noise and stared malignantly at Rhodri who carried on with his tirade quite undeterred.

"And don't you stare at me like that you bugger. This is my house and if you don't like it you can bloody well clear out "

It was an awful situation, but I just couldn't help myself. Rhodri who is always so gentle and calm was now ranting away at the top of his voice, cursing and swearing at the creature that had brought so much nastiness into his loving home. I had to laugh. This probably broke the tension of the moment and all the others joined in with me. When we came to compare notes later we all agreed that we thought the face of the evil spirit had also changed slightly and that before he left the room there had been a sort of wry smile on his lips too.

So there we were on a Thursday night; we had met the spirit/poltergeist of this house. Rhodri had given him a piece of his mind and the ghost/poltergeist had left the cold room suitably chastised with his tail between his legs. We all went home in a sombre mood - wondering what we had done. It's never a very wise thing for ordinary people like us to argue with a poltergeist.

But our poltergeist joined our circle on two other occasions and behaved reasonably well. He was grumpy, and he did a lot of growling, but so what! But he did answer our questions. He even told us his name: Harold Yates. The year, according to him was 1850 which we assumed was the year of his death. It appeared that in his life he had been some kind of animal dealer. He would buy about 20 cows in the Oswestry cattle mart and resell them to customer farmers along the Welsh border. This was how he had come to know of our Bala farm. From what he told us we deduced that Harold was a great womaniser. When his latest conquest had become pregnant he had denied all knowledge of the child.

Between two of his visits to us a spirit-woman called Mary came through. She was about 25-years-old and had been one of the maids at Bryntirion, Bala. Harold, who was possibly twice her age, appeared to her to have been a very rich and prosperous person and a very good catch. He had courted her for years and had pledged his troth to her before making her pregnant. Mary told us that when he'd heard that she had told the other maids that it was Harold Yates who was the father of her child, he had beaten her violently with a poker. He told her that he had no further use for her and that he was now going out with Martha the other maid.

When Harold next made contact Elwyn Edwards accused him of all these things. Harold was furious with us for "taking that little bitch Mary's word" against his. She was a liar to accuse him of being the father of her child just in order to get him to marry her. Elwyn Edwards then used great diplomacy with the 19th. century's Casanova.

'But true or not Harold," he had said, "you have to admit that in your day you were a bit a lad with the women weren't you?" We all thought that there were a semblance of a smile on Harold's face at this. He liked being called a lady's man.

Then Rhodri, in the face of the enemy, unable to hold back any longer burst out with the question: "You don't like me do you?" and the answer was prompt. "No I don't. I hate you"

"Why do you hate me?"

"I hate you because you are no good for her. She deserves someone better than you!"

Elwyn Edwards signalled that he would resume the questioning. He had very cleverly twigged a relationship the rest of us had failed to notice.

"You like Meiriona, Rhodri's wife, don't you Harold?" This resulted in a broad grin on his rather uncouth face.

"I have a feeling that you would like to marry Meiriona wouldn't you Harold"?

The grin broadened and there actually came out a real chuckle; Harold Yates was enjoying himself talking with Edwards about his latest ladylove, Meiriona, who was sitting at the table with us.

Amazingly enough after the whole thing was over Meiriona made a rather peculiar remark. "I have listened to all of you remarking how cold this middle room is. I have never said this before," she said, "but I have never in my life felt it cold in this particular room. I just went along with everyone else. I'd shut the doors if I saw them open like all of you did, but every time I went into the room it has always felt just as warm as any of the others'. She went on to say how Rhodri was always on about how they ought to do something about this room and how it smelt musty and damp and how it was spreading an unhealthy, stale, smell right through the rest of the house. "Well," said Meiriona, "I will confess to you now; when there was no one around I would quite often open the door of the middle room and pop my head inside. To me it always smelt of fresh roses." Harold obviously left nothing to chance when he "went a'courting."

But our third meeting with Harold was to become our crunch meeting. Harold was now being evasive about the date and manner of his death and refused to tell us where of when he had been buried. Suddenly Elwyn Edwards said to him; "You haven't crossed have you?" and Harold nodded his head in sad agreement. I could have kicked myself for not having thought of this before. It was so obvious. It had been staring at us every time we had spoken to him. Harold Yates was an earth-bound spirit. He had died in or around 1850 and had been hanging around Bryntirion for the last 150 years cursing, swearing and telling lies, and on top of everything else making Rhodri's life a complete misery. The amazing thing about his confession - that he hadn't crossed - was that he *knew* he hadn't crossed. I have only met a very few spirits that have been earth-bound (Most spirits just flutter back and forth from the other side to this world and back again). None of the earth-bound spirits I have come across have known they were dead. They either didn't know they were dead, or they had very conveniently "forgotten." They remained on earth carrying on doing their own thing very much as they had done before they died. One old chap who was a publican in Denbigh and who had died 30 earlier and who was still tending the bar at his hostelry [now converted into a dwelling house] nearly blew his top when I broke the news to him that he was, in fact, dead. It was like the John Cleese 'Dead Parrot' episode from the *Monty Python* comedy series. "You're dead!" I'd say; "No I'm not!" he'd answer. "You've fallen off your perch old boy". "Untrue, I'm only resting" etc. He called me all the names under the sun. But Harold was different from these others. Harold *knew* that he was dead and that he should have crossed but hadn't. Once Edwards starts on his inquisition there is no let up. "Didn't you want to cross?"

"No."

"Why not? Everyone else wants to cross"

"I was afraid."

It was at this point that I was called into the picture possibly in deference to my clerical collar. "Harold!" I said: "I am a priest. Tell me why you were too afraid to cross?"

"It was because I felt guilty," said Harold in a rather new hushed voice. The old parson then began to deliver his series of sermons to Harold on the "Love of God" and on the "Forgiveness of God," but Harold, unlike my more polite parishioners, cut across me and asked: "Will *she* be there then?"

We all took it that he meant Mary, the mother of his child. At this moment Mary walked into the room holding little Kate's hand. The last we saw was the three of them walking away together holding hands. Mary had come to fetch the man who 150 years previously had beaten so horrifically her with a poker.

Most disciplines, sciences in particular, have their own rules and definitions. Astronomers can, in a matter of seconds, give the high tide time for any day in the year 2011 just by using a recognised formula. Mathematicians have their safe and certain theorems that are constant. "In a right angled triangle the square on the hypotenuse is equal to the sum of the squares on the other two sides." Any mathematician can shout this out, or relay it on his *e.mail*, and there is not another mathematician in the world that will disagree with him. But in my ghostology researches there are no such theorems or constants; I have to make them up. I have already mentioned my theorem 1. Viz: *No spirit can manifest himself on earth without the aid of two mediums the one on the spirit side, and another on the earth side to open the door for him.* The second theorem I have concocted concerns poltergeists. Theorem 2. Viz: *"A poltergeist is a spirit who possesses some facets of human qualities, and can perform some human tasks or task.'*

Our Harold was most certainly a spirit. He had been born more than 150 years ago. He exhibited many spirit traits. He could change the temperature of the place where he roamed. His room was known as the cold room to everyone except Meiriona who recognised it as a warm room; a room smelling of sweet roses. He could remove and hide Rhodri's tobacco and his tools at will, and apparently so Rhodri told us, he could also move his furniture to the middle of the room and move it back again. Very much along the lines of what the old chap in Anglesey used to do to celebrate the birth of a child by re-arranging the library. No one seemed to know what Harold had to celebrate – certainly not the birth of his illegitimate child.

I forgot to ask Rhodri if he had had stones thrown at him - by his rival for Meiriona's hand - whilst he was out with the sheep. All poltergeists love throwing things. I would be surprised if Rhodri hadn't received a missile or two on the sly.

But it's not just stones they throw – it's anything they can lay hands on. There is a farm not very far from where I live where they seem to have been entertaining a poltergeist for years upon years. He performs about once a year. He has an orgy of throwing and of breaking crockery. The farmer and his wife are getting on for their seventies. This crockery breaking has been going on ever since they got married nearly fifty years ago and since, "she" the wife, came to live in the farm as a new bride. They have also noticed that it only "her" crockery that is broken - the crockery she has bought, or brought with her at the time of her wedding. Never "his" crockery that had been his parents before she came.

And the breakages are strange. No thief or vandal could ever break a piece of crockery as a poltergeist does. They have seen their best Staffordshire plate hurled against the wall at great speed, stop mid air and then float gently to the floor shattered, but the entire pieces jig-sawing together to make it appear as if still intact. It is only when touched that it disintegrates into myriad of a thousand parts.

Many have reported that crockery smashed to smithereens one day has been found the next day beautifully intact again.

I once saw a broom handle in a room vandalised by a poltergeist. It was lying on the floor and seemed to be the only object in the whole room that had not been shattered. When I tried to pick it up it had been shattered into thousands of match-like splinters and all placed together so meticulously that the handle seemed intact. It would have taken a very clever human a lifetime to complete such a task. The poltergeist had managed it, and a great deal more breakages, in just the two hours the householders had been out shopping.

So it certainly seems to me that a poltergeist, when he performs human actions, adds to them a little spirit power or spirit art. He leaves his stamp on his work very much as the old builders left their mason marks on their creations. Or better still his work resembles paint-tins advertised as "White with a touch of pink." So poltergeist actions can be described at "human with a touch of spirit." I have not, as yet, formulated my third ghostology theorem!

Without the shadow of a doubt Harold was a true-blue poltergeist. I never established which member of the family he derived his energy elixir from. There were the rather "sensitive" children in the house, but they seemed too involved with their own spirit adventures to have even noticed Harold.

I can only assume that it was poor maligned Rhodri who was supplying rival Harold with the wherewithal to continue plaguing him. Rhodri would be tamping mad if I were to tell him that I thought he was possibly the life sustainer of the "*bastard*" who seemed to have taken over his house.

Harold was as unpleasant and boorish in death as he appeared to have been in life. But even he had one person who loved him. Mary, and her little daughter, were able to return to Bryntirion after Elwyn had opened the door for them and take the old misery back with them to *Summerland*. Mary seemed a nice girl. She will quite probably be able to sort out her Harold given time.

But the one in the next chapter seems quite unredeemable - or he would be if we didn't have a God of all-encompassing love.

Chapter Eight

THE ENFIELD POLTERGEIST

Mrs Peggy Harper and her four children Rose (13), Janet (11), Pete (10) and Jimmy (7) lived at 48 Wood Lane, Enfield, London in the 1970's. Peggy's husband, the father of the children, had walked out earlier. There had been a great deal of domestic strife in the house before he had left. This, no doubt, had caused great stress within the family.

Mrs Harper however was a strong character and her children were intelligent and, if anything, precocious. The Council had placed Pete in one of their Boarding Schools for slow learners, but it seems that only the Council knew the reason why. Pete came home at weekends and for holidays.

Things were just beginning to settle down after dad's departure when Pete and Rose began to hear strange knockings in the house. They called their mother. The knockings were followed by strange shuffling sounds. Furniture then began to move; the chest of drawers in their bedroom began to move slowly from one end of the room to the other.

Peggy Harper decided this was enough. They all grabbed their nightclothes and beat a retreat to beg shelter with their very kind next door neighbour – Victor and Peggy Nottingham (or 'Peggy next door'). Vic and his son went back to the Harper household to investigate; they returned convinced the house was haunted. The date of this first of many retreats to the next door property is carefully recorded as "Half past nine on the evening of August 31st 1977."

This was the beginning of 14 months of a most tortuous and turbulent time for the Harper family.

When morning came Peggy Harper rang the police. Two police officers duly called and the new intruder to the Harper household gave them both a wonderful demonstration of his psychic powers. The policemen admitted they had not encountered anything like this before. They made notes and they left declaring, quite correctly, that no crime had been committed and that this was no police matter. They were very kind, but quite unable to help. Mrs Harper then turned for help to the '*Daily Mirror'* newspaper. George Fallows, one of Fleet Street's most experienced reporters was despatched to investigate. He said it was beyond doubt a poltergeist, and that he was going to phone the Society for Psychical Research, the only people he knew who had any kind of knowledge about these things. Poor Mrs Harper is reported to have fainted when she heard this.

Living a few miles from the Harper's was a newly enrolled member of the Society for Psychical Research. He was a Mr Maurice Grosse, an inventor of electrical gadgets, and a director of his own flourishing engineering business. His daughter, Janet Grosse, who had also been a newspaper reporter, had been killed, aged 22, in 1976. All sorts of coincidences, -and what could only be called psychic phenomena - happened within the Grosse family in the wake of her death. Her father became convinced that she was trying to make contact with them from beyond the grave. It was possibly his determination to help his daughter that convinced him join SPR. And he became a very active member indeed. There is some evidence that he rather pestered the case-secretary of the Society for a chance to do some research and some practical work. Within an hour of the SPR receiving the call from the *Mirror* newspaper, Maurice Grosse was given the task of investigating what was to become the most infamous poltergeist case ever known in Britain. Within minutes the anxious investigator was on his way.

I am convinced that no family in trouble could ever have been allocated a better, kinder, or more loyal friend than Maurice Grosse. He seemed to have been there every single day; there was never a mention of holidays or extra work at the office. He spent hours of his time at the Enfield home giving his full-time support to the family. He did return to his own home to sleep, but was always ready to rush back to the Harper's rescue even in the middle the night whenever summoned.

Within weeks another seemingly delightful person - Guy Lyon Playfair - joined Grosse. Playfair was the author of a great number of paranormal books. He had also written about the way that poltergeists in Brazil, a country that seemed to abound in such creatures, were treated. I am convinced that without the invaluable support of these two men the Harper's would have had to move house or would all have been driven insane by the activity of the beast spirit that had usurped their home.

As it was Janet, the 11-year-old daughter, had to spend three months in a psychiatric hospital during the investigations, which were to follow. Playfair wrote his famous book about the events that were to take place.

The book is called 'This House is Haunted' and was published by Souvenir Press Ltd in 1980. Normally I report only the psychic carryings on at which I have been present and have taken an active part or where I have personally verified others' reports. Here I rely on the meticulous report of Playfair, and on the countless reports written in newspapers and other books about this case, which at the time caught the imagination of the country.

My friends John and Ann Spencer in their jointly authored *'Encyclopaedia of Ghosts and Spirits'*, describe the case of the Enfield Poltergeist as "probably the most thoroughly investigated in Britain if not in Western Europe." The Spencers could be right when they say the house was thoroughly investigated, but only if they mean by this that every single fact was noted and carefully chronicled. But one has the impression that the investigators were acting more as observers than as people determined to bring the whole dreary saga to an end. I was not persuaded it should ever have been claimed to be the most efficient of investigations and certainly not the most humane. The whole miserable occurrence went on without a break from the night of the August 31st. 1977, when the family heard their first loud banging, until 'The Thing' was banished from the house by a young Dutch medium Dono Gmelig Meyling in October the following year.

As I read the story my heart bled for the poor, long suffering, Harper family having to live with this horrible vile 'Thing' for 14 months. Mrs Harper deserved a medal in the Queen's Honours list; her children were so brave, so resilient, and so very patient. Their home was not only invaded by the two kind honorary investigators but by a legion of so called experts who traipsed in and out at all hours of the day and night during this long period.

Maurice Grosse, the chief investigator, appears not to have had any training or experience in this kind of work. He had offered himself to the Society for Psychical Research to carry out fieldwork. True he was a member of the SPR but that in itself it is no prerequisite, and certainly no qualification for meddling with poltergeists. There are, I am told, a great number of SPR members whose only contact with the paranormal is what they read in books and reports. However Maurice Grosse was sent in at the very deepest end to solve the Great Enfield Mystery. His partner, who seems to have been a delightful and gentle fellow, was Guy Lyon Playfair. He was a writer. But one has the impression his writings were about cases he had perhaps witnessed in Brazil not cases he had personally investigated. Here again was a kind-hearted soul dabbling in something completely out of his league.

I am convinced, however, that these two kind men were welcomed with open arms by the Harper's in their distress. More important than anything they seemed to know the enemy; they confirmed that he was what the *Daily Mirror* reporter had described - a poltergeist. This, at a stroke, would have taken away the worst fear of all; fear of the unknown.

'The Thing' that came into their house on the evening of the 31st of August now at least had a name. It was something that was known to exist. It was something other families had experienced.

Soon, however, the thing with a name began to take more liberties. The noises it made grew louder especially during the night. Missiles were being thrown through the air at tremendous speed. The little family was terrified. Every single action of the 'Thing' was carefully recorded. Maurice

147

Grosse very wisely asked Mrs Harper if she would assist their research by keeping her own records. It proved to be good therapy for her. Within the first four months of their being in the house 1,500 paranormal incidents had been recorded. It appears that marbles and pieces of Lego were the favourite missiles of 'The Thing'. These were thrown at speed on to the walls but when they fell to the ground they neither bounced nor rolled; they just plopped and stayed exactly where they had fallen. This is something which is quite usual in polteristic targeting. Every throw was meticulously reported by the two investigators and carefully recorded in the book of events. Measurements are given.

'At five past ten a marble came whizzing towards him apparently out of nowhere …'

Playfair does warn in the introduction to his book that the reader might find parts of the book rather dull. The book itself is a fascinating read and anything but dull, but I have to agree with the author that some of the repeated statistics were, indeed, to become rather tedious. Every single tumble that a certain chair in the bedroom took was carefully recorded; every journey that the chest of drawers in the bedroom made was meticulously measured from wall to wall and carefully noted.

The two investigators, possibly because they themselves lacked the necessary experience, proceeded to call in a legion of experts. A physicist came with an array of meters. Expert hypnotists were called in, newspaper and television reporters trampled over the house, and college professors of various disciplines were in an out of the property like yo-yos … all doing their own thing, and writing their own lengthy reports and observations. And still 'The Thing ' continued to rule the roost in Wood Lane, dictating his own terms and conditions, and terrifying the Harper family.

Within a fortnight of the two investigators moving in (on Sept 17th) Maurice Barbanell, the prince of mediums, and the editor of *Psychic News* wrote to say;

"I think it strange that no one has thought of calling a medium to solve this mystery."

He went on to say that, "Mediums are the only real psychic experts in this field."

I felt a little happier that at last the two investigators had been told about mediums and their special gifts. But nothing happened; certainly not for some time and many more reams of 'evidence' for inclusion in their book. Mediums were, eventually, called in many months later and interestingly enough it is a medium who in the end sends 'The Thing' packing. But Maurice Gross seems to have been allergic to mediums. Playfair, I suspect, had to plead with his colleague before being allowed to introduce members of the medium fraternity into the house. Grosse is all for calling in more scientific experts, psychologists and physicists, speech therapist *et al.* But not mediums. I have wondered if this had anything to do with his being a Jew by religion. The Book of Deuteronomy which he would have studied and would know so well as a practising Jew, does carry the warning: *"Let no one be among you who practises divination or sorcery, interprets omens, engages in witchcraft or casts spells, or who is a medium or spiritist or who consults the dead ... etc"*

There is no such pronouncement against having dealings with psychologists or physicists or speech therapists.

Half way through the investigation a Professor Hasted, wisely I thought, suggested that they should challenge 'The Thing'. I remembered how our poltergeist, Harold, had been challenged spontaneously by farmer Rhodri. The minute Farmer Rhodri caught sight of his tormenting poltergeist in his house he leapt to his feet with fists shaking and confronted it head-on bellowing: "I know you, you bugger. It's you that's been stealing my tobacco and hiding my tools," and warning old Harold "Don't you glare at me you bastard. This is my house and if you don't like it you can bloody well go somewhere else!" And sure enough three weeks later our Welsh 'Thing' packed its bags and took leave of the farmhouse home in Bala where it had lived for years. I kept thinking that someone should be telling this 'Thing' at Enfield where to get off instead of pandering to him. But no one did. I can only recall from the account one wish of his which was denied him. 'The Thing' had demanded for music to be played for him at one o'clock in the morning. They did, at this point, have the courage to tell him he would have to wait until a more reasonable hour of the day and it seemed to take the admonishment on the chin. As I read the book *"This House is Haunted"* I kept finding myself repeating to myself: "When are you two people going to call in a medium?"

After several months both family and investigators began to see apparitions, or ghosts, of elderly men around the house.

(They called these apparitions 'entities'. They all seemed shy of using the words 'ghosts' or 'spirits'.) But they did give their entities names. They called them 'Charlie' and 'Joe'. The one was thought to have been the man who had lived in the house before the Harpers moved in and the other was thought to be old grandpa Nottingham, from next door, who had died a few years previously.

I felt that the investigators were spending a great deal of their time and energy trying to connect 'The Thing' with one or other, or both, of these old spirit gentlemen. This made me feel just a little bit nervous. I began to have new doubts as to whether our specialists had ever really been inside a haunted house before. For whenever our small team is called to sort out an unruly spirit, it is often difficult to filter out the particular 'ghost' that is in need of a spot of discipline and so very easy to be distracted by the actions of other quite unconnected spirits.

I remember in one house where we were particularly anxious to contact an old bishop of Bath and Wells from the 1200's. We had already had one most illuminating chat with the bishop some weeks previously and we were waiting for him to come back. We have a general rule that we never call a spirit. It is always "We won't call you; you call us." We'd all taken our places and were waiting when instead of the bishop our old spirit-friend Richard Wynne shuffled in. We had spoken to him many times before. Tonight it was different.

The old man was so very sad. He told us he was 86-years-of-age and that he had died in 1874. From time to time he would wipe a tear from his eyes. We asked him why he was so sad. Elwyn told us that he could see him driving a horse-drawn hearse to a church on which was laid the small coffin of a child. He had, apparently, been an undertaker by trade. He told us that all his children had died before reaching adulthood. His wife had blamed him for bringing diseases into the house from the dead bodies he had handled in preparation for burials.

I have come to the conclusion over many years that practically every house in Britain has its own little group of ghosts hopping in an out. Charlie and Joe probably had no connection whatsoever with 'The Thing'. They were just part of the normal household compliment of ghosts and were probably just as annoyed, even disgusted, about 'The Thing's' antics as was everyone else.

Somewhere around page 100 of the book 'The Thing' discovers that he has a voice; a deep guttural voice that shouted obscene things in short staccato sentences. A voice that seemed to be in keeping with his filthy habit of spreading human excreta on the floors and walls and bathroom taps in the house. He made the rules to please himself. He would only speak and answer questions when the girls were in the room with him and even then only when the bedroom door was closed. I was amazed. Dependent as Mrs Harper was on the company of her two knights-in-armour that she even countenanced allowing her two girls to be alone with the monster in a room behind a closed door. But that was how he wanted it.

If the men left the door a fraction open the voice would bellow at them "SHUT THE BLOODY DOOR!" and they humbly obeyed whereas my friend Rhodri would have retorted, "*Shut the bloody thing yourself ... on your way out!*"

And then more often than not it was just a string of four-letter words. But amazingly it seems that the investigators' main concern from this point onwards was whether this horrible voice and the obscene words were coming out of little Janet's mouth or from the unseen mouth of the 'Thing'. They now began to accuse poor Janet of playing tricks. The words, and the hatred behind the words, were obviously not the words or the thoughts of an eleven-year-old girl but tests had to be carried out; a laryngometer was brought into the house. Common sense was not enough to these intrepid SPR investigators; scientific proof had to be found. Whether the voices came from the monster's home-made voicebox or whether he was using Janet's vocal cords was of no significance. But it was of great significance to the investigators. At one stage they taped Janet's lips to make sure that she was not playing tricks on them. I had the distinct impression that the Harper's had found for themselves and in their time of great need, two excellent and faithful friends; two excellent researchers and chroniclers, but unfortunately two men who lacked neither knowledge nor experience, nor certainly the courage to tackle the horrible 'Thing' in the way it should have been tackled.

In my day I have listened to an earth-bound spirit speaking perfect Welsh using the mouth and the vocal gearbox of a monoglot English-speaking medium. I have heard the ghost of a Russian forestry worker speaking through a Welsh medium in Russian. When, on the other hand, spirits prefer using the vocal chords of my friend Elwyn their voices sound, as one might expect, rather similar to Elwyn's natural voice. But there again Elwyn is a rather exceptional sensitive. Whose physical voice box is being utilised is not important. What is important is the 'person' using it. But the Enfield investigators even called in speech therapists to see if it was possible for a girl of eleven to speak in the deep guttural tones of the 'The Thing' without injuring her own vocal chords. I'm not surprised that she eventually needed psychiatric help.

By this time Janet was being frequently dragged out of her bed by the 'Thing' and flung, still sleeping, under the bed or on to the top of the radio. The distance each time carefully measured and noted by the chroniclers as '8 feet'.

By the time we come to page 111 Janet has most definitely been possessed by 'The Thing'. She has become a thin, pale, limp and a listless child, spending most of her time lying down whimpering. I was almost shouting as I read the book, "Get a medium to her you clowns or she'll die on you." It seemed fortuitous that at this time two mediums whom Playfair had met in Brazil were in London attending a conference. They were Luiz Gasparetto and Elsie Dubugras. Playfair and Grosse had a little discussion whether or not invite them to Enfield. As a result any event Playfair called them in and they attended the house for a short session with Janet. Luiz got hold of Janet as she lay whimpering on the settee. He shouted at her: "Listen you. We've had enough or your nonsense. I know you can understand me. Now get out of her. Get out of her NOW!" The Brazilians were only able to stay in Enfield a couple of hours and yet Playfair, the accurate chronicler, writes that within minutes Janet was her own normal self again. The two experienced mediums from Brazil had used against 'TheThing', the same bullying tactics that Rhodri, my farmer friend, had used to get rid of his 'thorn in the flesh'. Rhodri had been rather cruder in his instructions than the Brazilian mediums. He had thundered: "You remember that this is my house you bastard, and if you don't like it here you can bloody well find somewhere else!" And that also had worked.

By page 211 things are really bad again. Her tormentor no longer possesses Janet but she is still being thrown about, being denied the sleep so necessary to a child of her age. In fact, she was actually being denied her 'childhood' by this monster thing. She is now so weak that she is in need of hospitalisation and psychiatric care. Once again the two investigators have a little *tête-à-tête* and they agree to call in another medium. His name is Gary Sherrick, by trade a Hackney taxi driver. He must have been a good fellow. He tells Playfair that if he agrees to attend he cannot afford the time to make more than one visit. He also tells the duo that he would not accept any payment for his services; he considered that he had had been given a gift by God and that it would not be honest for him to charge others for the use of that gift.

Sherrick remained in the house for only a very short time. He told Janet that he recognised in her a person who had been endowed with very strong psychic powers. His advice to her was that she should go to someone who could teach her how to develop these mediumistic abilities. His message was very simple; "You have the power within yourself my dear to get rid of this 'Thing' which is so troubling your family. All you need is someone who can teach you how use your sensitiveness." This was almost word for word what the other mediums, Mr and Mrs Shaw had said during an earlier visit. I put my book down and clapped my hands.

A few years ago Elwyn and I had been called to the home of a young married woman in Bangor who was having great trouble with unidentified things that were troubling her. Her husband was a factory worker who had to work nights every fourth week of the month. On nights during these fourth weeks when she slept on her own in the house, she would be woken in the middle of the night. Her bed would be rocked violently and all around her there would be voices, as if made by hundreds of goblins jeering and taunting her. Elwyn and I called at the house where her mother, sister and her best friend joined us. Elwyn immediately discovered that this young woman had tremendous psychic power. I remember how we sat in a circle and all joined hands together. Within seconds Elwyn and the young woman, holding each other's hands, were both thrown into the air as if they had suffered a severe electric shock. I had chosen to hold the hands of the mother and the best friend and suffered no harm. When Elwyn recovered he told our young client exactly what the Enfield taxi driver had told Janet. You've got terrific power young lady. You have far more psychic power that I have. I now know why your bed is rocking and why you hear these spirit voices mocking you. The spirits around you know you have this power and that you are not using it. They want you to exploit it to the full. They want to show themselves to others through you'. Elwyn then went on to tell her that as a gifted sensitive she would go through life, "always seeing things that other people didn't see" and "hear things other people didn't hear." He very carefully explained to her that people like he and she, who had this wonderful gift of being able to help spirits from the beyond, also needed their own space and time off just as doctors and nurses do. They must pattern their lives, keep set surgery hours, open an appointments book and make it clear to spirit clients that there is a time and a place for everything, and that it is the medium who sets these times and places and not the patients.

Every time I have commended a spiritualist healer for his or her gift of healing they have said to me "But you *also* have this gift." These people seem to believe that we all have this sensitive psychic gift of peering into worlds beyond and of using paranormal powers to heal others and ourselves. They also say of those of us who are no longer able to heal, or dowse for water or things lost, or to communicate with the spirits of the departed, that we did have these gifts at one time. But, they say, because we didn't know we had them we didn't use them, and like all other things not used they had become rusty and useless. That is their firm belief. I find it difficult to accept that these special gifts of God are evenly distributed amongst His people. God is no Marxist, after all God's other gifts are not equally shared. Some people are able to paint and even earn their living by their gift of painting; some of us are so lacking in this gift that we are not even able to draw an egg.   Some are able to compose beautiful music; others are so tone deaf they cannot enjoy listening to good opera.

No.   While I might envy them, I bid all sensitives enjoyment of the gifts bestowed on them, alone, by God. These are special gifts given to very special people.

"*This House is Haunted*" has 288 pages and I was now nearing the end of the book. No one seemed to have taken the advice of the medium who had proposed that Janet should have mediumship instruction.   Things were as bad as they ever had been in the house. Janet had spent three months as a patient in a psychiatric hospital and 'The Thing' had just continued as before. Brave, patient, Mrs Harper was at her wits end. Then at the darkest hour it happened on page 265. A Dutch journalist named Peter Liefhebber asked if he could come to the house in Enfield and bring with him a young medium called Dono Gmelig-Meyling with him.   Peter Liefhebber explained that the young medium was very highly thought of in the Netherlands. He went on to say of him that he was also a very good clairvoyant and also a healer.   (I liked the sound of all this because mediums I have worked with all seem to have had this tri-talent,) Peter was then asked it he thought his young friend, Dono, could beat 'TheThing'. He replied, quite casually, that he was quite sure he could. He had only recently told two rather violent Dutch poltergeists where they could get off. When Dono arrived, Playfair asked him how he proposed to end the Enfield case.

His reply was simple and assuring. "First," he said, "I will have to cure the people in the house." Then he described to Playfair how we all carry a certain amount of energy inside our bodies, as if in containers. Sometimes, but not often, these containers begin to leak and just as sharks smell blood and gravitate towards it, so certain spirits are attracted to this leaking energy from the human body and gravitate towards that. These become poltergeists and by using this energy from a human person are able to perform all the useless, sometimes mischievous, and at other times horrible, crude and wicked things the 'The Thing' had been carrying out. So the first thing to do, according to the young medium, was to cure the people in the house; stop the leakage of energy from their bodies and starve the poltergeist. I rubbed my hands with glee. After 14 months of sheer torture for the little Harper family we appeared, at last, to be making progress. At this point Playfair concedes that this is virtually what the other mediums had also said. But Dono wasn't here just to give advice. Dono was a 'hands on' specialist.

He would go into trance. He would see things and persons others were unable to see. He would describe the people he saw in exactly the same way Elwyn would describe his people to us, and then he'd invite their comments. Just as I had expected, one focus-person began to stand out in his mind. He could see a young woman, he said, of about 24 years of age. Did any of them know her? He told them that he could only see her vaguely but her age, he said, was 24 years. This at least was clearly impressed on his mind. This particular girl, he said, had been involved in an accident. She seemed to be close to Janet. Did anyone know a girl of 24 who had died; probably killed in an accident?

At this point Grosse put his hand up. "I had a daughter called Janet," he said. "She was 22 years old when she was killed in a motor-cycle accident." He then added; "She would have been 24 today had she lived." At this point Dono seemed to shut the book. He just said: "Well, that's it. It's your daughter."

At this stage I felt as I often do when I have been watching a *Poirot* whodunit or a Ruth Rendell mystery on telly. Just before the end I sort of close my eyes and wander off a little, and then the story comes to an abrupt end to make room for the ten o'clock news. *"It's the butler what done it!"*

Similarly, I woke up with a jolt when I read of Dono saying, "Well that's it. It's your daughter." It was all so sudden so abrupt. Nothing, it seems, could have led the plot so far to this conclusion. I wasn't quite clear what he meant. Was he suggesting that the dead girl, Janet Grosse, the journalist, was the poltergeist? There were still about six pages left to read. I read them carefully to see if I could find an answer. These pages told me that Maurice Grosse was also a worried man, and so was Playfair. Was Dodo suggesting that Grosse had taken the spirit of his daughter with him to this house like a person carries the 'flu virus into the home of another? How could the death of his daughter Janet have involved the little Harper family is so much trouble? Maurice Grosse and Guy Lyon Playfair were also struggling with the ending of this Horror Film as much as I was. Playfair suggests to Grosse that Dodo had merely included his daughter, Janet, as one of the many other apparitions that had been seen in the house. Many of these, he said, were nice people as no doubt had been his daughter - there had been the little boy that John Burcombe had thought could have been his little brother. Then there had been the nice old man who had just been sitting quietly at the table, and the other old man whom Victor Nottingham thought could well have been his grandfather.

I had closed the book and put it back on its shelf but I was still compelled to think about it.

Maurice Grosse couldn't possibly have introduced 'The Thing' into 48 Wood Lane. 'The Thing' had been active in this house when the police were called in and the reporter from the *Daily Mirror* reported it to the SPR before Maurice Grosse had ever heard of it. I could only think that Janet Grosse (deceased) had found her way there because her father was there. She had followed him. Janet in her life had also been a reporter and a very inquisitive reporter at that according to all accounts. She was also, I would think, in this house for a purpose. I am reminded of my visit to see Winnie Marshall and how Winnie, after smiling genially over my left shoulder, would remark on what a nice man my father was. She had then told me that every time I had called at her house, my father would have been with me and that he was my guide. Janet Grosse must have known how badly her poor father needed help. She knew, bless him, that he was trying to tackle the most awful spirit beast in the land without an ounce of training or experience. She knew he was under great stress. She must have been crying out to him, as was I,

"Daddy please call a medium! It is a medium this little family needs more than anything!" Dono had said that Janet Grosse, the twenty four year-old girl he could see, had been involved with Janet, the Harper daughter.

That explained something else to me. I had often wondered how this little girl of 11 managed to live through her ordeal. She had been the focus throughout. She was dragged out of her bed almost nightly and thrown about the room, landing some nights balanced on top of her small radio. She was so tired that she would continue to sleep in this uncomfortable position. For a long time she had also been under suspicion that she was the perpetrator of all the trouble. Throughout the reading of the book I had almost been afraid of turning a page lest I find that Janet had been found dead. I would say, with hindsight, that she possibly didn't die because Janet Grosse was there looking after her. Janet, her spirit-guide.

The ending to this nightmarish saga came abruptly. I was rather disappointed that Playfair had not, like my old friend *Poirot*, spent a quiet twenty pages or more winding down the story; explaining how it had all come about. But the end that matters comes with the knowledge that, after 14 months of nightmare, this horrible lump of nastiness had been banished from the lives of this lovely little family and their friends.

The story of the Enfield poltergeist seems more horrible than anything that could be created by a Hollywood film company; and there have been a few of them including the true '*Emityville*' drama which still sends shudders up the spine. My hands felt clammy as I read the *This House is*

Haunted and I felt ill at ease and disturbed even describing the events second hand.

One has to ask if this disgusting and appalling poltergeist was a human being before he became a poltergeist and if so, whatever kind of a human person would he have been in his prior life on earth? Most certainly an arch-neighbour from hell.

Here I think I have to reassure my readers in very much the same way as Nick Ross, the presenter of *Crimewatch UK* reassures his viewers. He ends his programme with words along the lines of: "Please don't be too worried by what you have seen tonight. Crime is not always as hideous as we have shown you and there isn't so much of it. We have shown you the very worst examples. Do sleep well." I say very much the same to my readers. This Enfield beast was possibly the most horrible that has been experienced in this country. Many poltergeists are bad and vicious and those dealing with them know the risks they take. It is never pleasant dealing with this type of spirit, but having said that, one has to admit that they are not *all* bad. Harold, my own poltergeist in the farm in Bala, was not a choice-character; not the sort of type a normal person would want as a partner or a mate. I would certainly not want him as a son-in-law. He was a wife beater, a braggart, a womaniser and a cheat. He was also a coward; he wouldn't 'cross over' for fear that little Mary who he'd bludgeoned would be there to embarrass him. But he did have the grace to smile a little when Rhodri told him off and he did have the decency to show some remorse. Our Enfield chap would have spat obscenities at Rhodri.

Others which follow are equally innocent in comparison with the Enfield lout. 'Pete', the Cardiff poltergeist, loved company, enjoyed playing games and was always willing to please. He even provided money for his rent. The little boy poltergeist just behaved as all little boys do. The worse thing he could think of doing was throwing stink bombs he had bought in Llandudno. As I have already mentioned, I know of a hair salon, not very far from where I live, which also plays host to a poltergeist; its proprietoress would not part with this customer gimmick for all the tea in china. The salon's pet poltergeist wafts from one customer to the other giving a little tug to a curl here and a bob there. He throws a pair of scissors into the air and let's them drop gently into the lap of a chosen customer. He is so harmless that the customers leave disappointed when it's his day off.

But the general rule is, keep away from poltergeists if you possibly can. And it is quite natural, when one considers the callousness and the selfishness of the Enfield poltergeist, to ask what kind of a human being would, after death, chose to be so brutal and so selfish.

There are so many good people in the world with so many kind acts perpetrated every minute of the day. But there are also a very tiny minority of evil men and women in the world we live in. We tend to make excuses for them; that it is their upbringing which has made them what they are. Robbed of love they cannot give love. That may be so, but I have come to the conclusion that there still are, for whatever reason, people who are sadistically evil. They take pleasure hurting others.

I remember reading in my local paper, the *Daily Post*, some years ago how three vile young men had been arrested after breaking into a North Wales Church. They had vandalised the church and, as a final act of spite against the people who worshipped there, the three of them had gone and urinated against the holy altar. In court later they pleaded they had been drunk … but they were not too drunk to know that the altar of a church was the most holy of places for the worshippers and that it is there that Christians congregate to receive the body and the blood of their Lord. Theirs was an act worthy of the Poltergeist of Enfield himself. As I read the account of their blasphemy I couldn't help feeling that three men who could perform such an abomination in life have the potential to make awesomely evil poltergeists in death.

Chapter Nine

'PETE' OF CARDIFF

Some years ago I was invited by a television production company to travel to Cardiff to give, on camera, my opinion of a ghost investigation that was being carried out in the city. There was the promise of liberal expenses and a large fee at the end of the day.

I caught the early train from Bangor and arrived in Cardiff mid-morning and once there was swept by taxi to a churchyard somewhere in the city. There the producer told me what it was all about. They were investigating a rather unusual ghost occurrence that had been going on for some months. He described the background. This particular ghost could, apparently, throw stones. As a matter of fact he seemed to spend most of his days throwing stones and there was, they said, a very real fear that one day someone might get hurt.

The producer wanted to know from me whether I thought this ghost was a special type of ghost; whether he was known by a special name and whether I was prepared to agree with him that there was a very real danger to members of the public if this spirit was allowed to carry on with it's indiscriminate stone-throwing. I replied to the whirring of cameras that, from what he had told me, I would say that it was a special type of ghost; a ghost to be defined as a poltergeist and that its stone-throwing posed very little danger to members of the public. I went on to tell them that these ghosts, in spite of their loudness and their extrovert behaviour, hardly ever caused injury to people. They seemed to have a natural talent for stone-throwing. They were expert target hitters. Some had been reputed to have hit a target that was round the corner from the place they were throwing! But when objects were thrown at humans they were invariably made to 'near miss' the target or fall lightly and gently on his person.

It became clear that this was not what the television production team wished to hear. The producer pulled out his chequebook made out a cheque to cover my expenses and fees and ordered a taxi to take me back to the station. The whole thing was over in a matter of five minutes. I am pretty certain that the notes the producer took of my interview and the interview he recorded on camera, were both stripped out and thrown in to the nearest litter bin after I had turned my back. When the film appeared on screen there was no mention of my little contribution. I had told them something they didn't want to know.

It was some months later before I discovered the person who had been invited by the SPR to investigate this particular Cardiff disturbances was my friend David Fontana, professor of parapsychology at Cardiff University College. Professor Fontana would in all probability have told the television people everything I had told them. But it was still worth offering me a fee plus expenses in the hope that I might say something contradictionary.

Nothing makes a television documentary more interesting than a good, slogging, disagreement between two so-called "experts'. Neither of us would oblige.

The story of the Cardiff poltergeist is very different from that of the Enfield horror. The Cardiff specimen was called 'Pete' by all who knew him. He was a stone thrower *par excellence*. David Fontana has kindly let me have a copy of his official report to the SPR. John and Ann Spencer, those prolific writers about all things paranormal and who had also visited Cardiff after the SPR report had been published, add a delightful little tit-bit to the story. In their book, *The Poltergeist Phenomenon* they say that when the locals came to hear about Pete "they would visit the yard where he lived.

They would arrive with bags full of stones to play with him. They also tell how, particularly, one old man came with a handful of stones. He was told to throw them at a certain corner of the yard where Pete had set up his throwing stand. The old man was absolutely thrilled when his marked stones where returned to him within a split second."

Pete the poltergeist had taken up residence in a place in Cardiff where there was a small engineering workshop and an adjoining retail shop. The business was owned jointly by Jim and his wife Ann, Paul, (Ann's brother) and his wife Yvonne. There were also a couple of workmen who acted as witnesses to Pete's activities.

It was in 1989 that the stone throwing all began. Stones were thrown against the roof of the workshop, and every morning the first job had to be the sweeping out of pebbles that had littered the inside of the buildings during the night. Jim the owner contacted the Society for Psychical Research to ask for help and advice. He was afraid that one of the stones could so easily hit and injure a customer or a passer-by. John Stiles, Honorary Cases Officer for the Society had written to David Fontana, professor of paranormal psychology at Cardiff University College, to ask if he would investigate the disturbance.

There followed months of frequent calls and meticulous investigation. I have no doubt that David Fontana enjoyed having a comparatively friendly poltergeist living on his very doorstep in Cardiff. 'Laboratory' conditions in the shadow of his office so to speak.

In his report David tells us that the poltergeist was fondly referred to as 'Pete' by all who came in contact with him. Pete's main hobby, in common with many others or his ilk, was throwing stones, bolts, nuts, coins and anything he could lay hands on. Workmen and customers would from time to time feel "Pete's missiles flying past them." Very few ever made contact and when they did, the projectiles seemed to have lost their velocity by the time they hit their target.

David describes Pete as a "*Reciprocal Poltergeist.*" Pete's maxim to all other throwers of missiles seemed to be, "Anything you can do I can do better." A stone thrown by a workman to the place known as Pete's haunt in the yard would be reciprocated. The men would mark some of their stones and it was found that these marked stones were the ones returned with split-second timing and pin-point accuracy. The popular target for Pete, and for the workmen, during lunch breaks was an empty artillery shell case in the yard. Every time a workman scored a hit there would be a metallic ping followed immediately by another made as Pete made it a draw. *'Love All'* so to speak. Professor Fontana reports how on one occasion a workman feigned to throw his stone but kept it in his hand. This action fooled Pete whose stone hit the target with just a solitary ping. "*Love-15*" to the workmen"

On one occasion when Jim was directing a customer in the shop to another part of the city he said to him, "If I had pen and paper I would draw a map of the route for you." Hardly had the words been spoken when a biro fell from the ceiling and a sheet of headed notepaper from the offices above floated gently on to his head. There is no doubt but that Pete wandered freely from one building to the other in the complex where he lived. He had also managed free access to the homes of the principle characters in his drama.

One of the workmen, knowing 'Pete's' interest in coins, asked him if he could find a sovereign for him. Immediately a Jubilee Crown fell at his feet. It was revealed later that the Jubilee Crown was one that had been removed from Jim, the boss's home. When the workman asked for more money three old pennies dated 1912 dropped from the sky.

On another occasion a paint-scraper disappeared for days. When it was returned it was red hot – just as if it had been heated with a blowlamp. But Pete's next best favourite toys after stones were carburettor floats. These floats had sharp needles embedded at each end.

These were found stuck to the ceilings of the shop and workshops and even to the walls and ceilings of the men's homes. On one occasion Jim and Paul were leaving the premises together. Just out of devilment Paul placed one float on a table by the door saying something like, "Move that then, you little blighter!" They were the last to leave. They locked up the shop and went off together. On their way home they stopped to buy cigarettes at a tobacconist. As Paul picked up his change he found a carburettor float amongst the coins. They rushed back to the shop only to find that the float left on the table by the door minutes earlier had disappeared.

On another occasion Paul found that a float had been pushed ever so gently inside his shirt.

The entire workforce, Professor Fontana, the customers and visiting salesmen all witnessed these phenomena. David Fontana lists 16 happening he personally witnessed, including his being hit by a stone and by a ball bearing. He says however that although the objects thrown appear to have travelled at great speed when they made contact their landing only seemed like a gentle touch.

After months of playing and teasing it seemed that Pete was beginning to tire. Kids do get bored. There were changes in the works. Alterations were carried out to the buildings; Jim changed his work partners. It all seemed a little too much for Pete and he appeared to be spending more time now at Paul's house than he did at the workplace. Paul, of course, had always been the focus of his activity.

Like every good lodger Pete insisted on paying his house-rent. Notes were found pinned to the walls of the house and odd coins left on the table. Sometimes it would amount to £15 in a month. No one seems to have asked where he got his money!

Then one day Paul saw him. He said that he saw a small boy sitting on a tall shelf in the workshop. On another occasion he saw a small boy dressed in short trousers and a peaked cap waving to him as if he was going away. Professor Fontana, after submitting his report to the SPR, was recalled a year later to witness the renewed activities of poltergeist Pete. I leave it to David to report what he saw through his eyes; those of an expert investigator.

"In my first report (April 1991) on what I termed "a responsive poltergeist (nicknamed "Pete' by witnesses) I mentioned the fact that although the phenomena witnessed by me had now ceased, some events of a different character had begun to occur and might provide material justifying a further article. These events have now continued sporadically for twelve months, and although lacking the evidential value of those previously reported they warrant recording in that, in two respects at least, they add significantly to the unusualness of the case.

Background

The setting of the case is a small light engineering workshop and retail premises situated in a small suburban shopping parade in South Wales. At the time of first writing the proprietor of the business (himself one of four witnesses) had succeeded in keeping matters from the press, but in July of last year his landlord informed a Welsh national newspaper which promptly sent a reporter to request an interview. The proprietor, referred to as Jim, in my last report (to avoid confusion I shall retain the pseudonyms used previously by me), agreed out of courtesy to speak to her and an illustrated article by her subsequently appeared in the newspaper concerned. This consisted of a cursory but a largely accurate summary of a few of the more spectacular phenomena, and although it attracted some local attention it proved relatively non-intrusive.

At the time of this visit I was out of the country, but apart from this and other absences abroad I have continued to visit the premises regularly and to keep a record of all ostensibly paranormal phenomena. The principal witnesses remain as in my first report, namely Jim, and his wife Ann, Ann's brother Paul, and Paul's wife Yvonne. All four are on the premises during working hours and currently there are no other employees. As in my first report all four witnesses express themselves prepared to give full descriptions of all relevant occurrences.

Current phenomena

The reciprocal stone throwing incidents, which were such a feature of the earlier phenomena, and which ceased on the rearrangement and structural alterations to the premises and Jim's dissolution of his partnership with a fifth witness, Michael, have not recurred. Nor have many of the other incidents detailed in my last report, which also ceased at or around this time. However, after a lull of some few weeks, during which time it was thought that all paranormal activity had finally ceased, I was summoned to the premises by an early morning telephone call in order to observe the results of disturbances that had happened overnight.

Similar disturbances occurred regularly for some weeks and on several occasions I visited the premises to witness the results before any attempt was made to clear them up. I list these in the order they made their first appearance.

1. Large amounts of grass seed and of granular fertiliser scattered over the floor and over the counter of the retail premises. These materials originated in polythene sacks positioned on the floor but since the surface of the counter was away from, and significantly above, the mouths of the sacks the activity of mice or some other animals could be ruled out as a possible explanation, even

were such livestock present (and there was no evidence that they were). All doors and windows were closed and firmly secured overnight and so draughts of air could also be ruled out as a possible explanation. In addition, the widely broadcast nature of the materials, which covered the length of the counter and a large area of the floor, would also discount any natural explanation. The impression, on the several occasions on which the phenomenon occurred, was that the materials had been thrown in large handfuls and with some force around the shop.

This scattering of grass seed and fertiliser took place for the most part during the night, when the premises were locked and nobody around. However, on one occasion, when Paul was serving a retail customer in broad daylight he observed what appeared to him as a sudden dark cloud of granular fertiliser above the customer's head, which then fell as a shower on the latter's head and shoulders, startling him so much that Paul reports he left without waiting to pick up his change.

2. Plates from a display on the shelves in the retail premises smashed on the floor overnight yet with the pieces arranged perfectly together instead of scattered apart, as would have been the case if they had fallen naturally.

3. The engine of a powerful commercial petrol mower found running in a fume filled workshop on Paul's opening up the premises on a Monday morning. I later checked that this mower required no less than

three separate operations in order to start it. The final one involving a pull-start achievable only by repeated brute physical force. There is therefore no possibility of its having started by its own volition, or of Paul, who was not in robust physical strength at the time, absent-mindedly starting it. The loudness of the engine ruled out the possibility of its having been left accidentally running when the premises were last vacated. Indeed even if it had been left running, the petrol in a full tank would have been insufficient to keep the motor operating for the 36 hours from Saturday evening to Monday morning.

4. Crude attempts (again overnight) to lay cutlery in place settings in the small kitchen at the rear of the premises, sometimes on the table, sometimes on the floor.

5. A carburettor float (such floats were a frequent focus of the activities described in my first report) impacting on a wall in front of Ann and Paul when they were standing on the pavement across the road from the shop. Both reported having their hands in their pockets at the time.

6. A carburettor float impacting with multiple ricochets off three of the walls of Paul's living room whilst he sat at home with his son.

7. A Rubric cube placed on a shelf in the workshop, regularly re-arranged overnight, and once moved to a different shelf.

8. Three-carburettor floats thrown through the open window of Paul's car while he waited for Yvonne

in a supermarket car park. (I have been unable to trace a witness to this event whom Paul says was sitting in an adjacent car at the time.)

9. The regular appearance of money over a period of some weeks. These events appear to have been in response to repeated requests to Pete by the four principal witnesses to "bring some money." In all over £70 appeared in this way primarily in the form of rolled up £5 notes pinned prominently (overnight whilst the premises were locked) to the ceiling by carburettor floats, or placed on the floor, or found (on no fewer than four occasions) by the principal witnesses in the street outside the shop. On two occasions, however, the money arrived in a different manner, once a £10 note was found pasted on the wet windscreen of Paul's car at the end of the afternoon, and once five one-pound coins violently struck his front door whilst he was crossing the darkened hallway. (In his account he reported the impression that they were flung "through' the door from outside, rather than simply rebounding from inside) With the exception of this last incident none of the money was seen to "arrive" by any of the witnesses.

10. Movement of objects. Yvonne's watch disappeared when placed at her side (though not under her direct observation) whilst she washed her hands in the kitchen, and was later found hanging on a hook in the shop. A more dramatic example happened late one afternoon when Paul, who was last to leave the premises, heard a crash from inside just as he was leaving the back entrance after locking the door

behind him. Shaken by the violence of the noise he sought the assistance of a shop-keeper from across the road and together they unlocked and entered the premises to find that a set of step ladders had been thrown, in company of several small objects, from the workshop through the connecting door and into the retail shop. A search of the premises (which contain few hiding places) established that no one was present.

None of the objects concerned in this second example had been touched until I had been called to inspect matters the following morning. From the position of the steps it was clear they could not have fallen by gravity from a position against the wall, and that they could not have displaced the other objects involved. I interviewed the shopkeeper who had accompanied Paul into the premise and he confirmed in every detail the account given by Paul.

11. The appearance on three occasions of an apparition apparently associated with the disturbances. On each occasion Paul was the only witness, although on the second of them Jim was also present. The three occasions were as follows:-

   a) On opening the workshop door at the start of the working day, Paul saw an apparition of a small boy aged about 12 years, sitting on one of the shelves near the ceiling in what in my first report I referred to as the "active" corner. Only the natural light thrown through the workshop door illuminated the room, but Paul noted that the boy was wearing short trousers and a peaked cap.

Apart from an oval shape there was however no face under the cap, and no outline of hands or bare knees. In spite of the strangeness of the sight Paul reported no fear, "In fact it was quite a pleasant experience as if seeing a real child." Paul called out, "Hello" and some such words as "What are you doing here?" whereupon a float was thrown at him from the active corner and the apparition vanished.

b) Paul and Jim were working together on a piece of machinery kneeling on the floor in the middle of the workshop and illuminated by full electric light. Paul once again caught sight of the apparition and at once called to Jim to "Look behind you," whereupon the apparition vanished and simultaneously a large stone struck the machinery on which the two men were working, shaking both of them.

c) Paul, who was last to leave the premises was making his way across the workshop towards the rear exit when he saw the apparition standing by the open door of the washroom and silhouetted in the electric light thrown from this room (the light from the workshop had been extinguished, but the light from the washroom was good). Again there were no obvious hands or face, and the figure which he estimates at about two and a half feet tall was again in short trousers and peaked cap, "braided down the sides as the caps worn by wolf-cubs used to be," appeared to be waving and "as if saying goodbye." This time Paul was deeply disturbed by the experience, and after

179

giving details found it difficult for some time afterwards to discuss any aspect of the apparition or of the other disturbances. (Not surprisingly, the newspaper report showed particular interest in this event, and carried an artist impression, based upon Jim's account of Paul's sightings)

d) The disappearance of a large rubber ball and a teddy kept in the workshop. Hearing sounds above the suspended ceiling in the workshop, Paul and Jim investigated and found both objects hidden away in the ceiling space. On reflection they consider that the sounds they heard were as of the rubber ball " being bounced up and down in place

Discussion

Although a frequent observer of the disturbances detailed above, I did not see any of them actually taking place. With the exception of incidents 5, 7, and 9, and the three incidents associated with the apparition, none of the witnesses saw them actually taking place either. Thus all of them are more open to normal explanations than many of the events detailed in my first report. Let me examine what form such explanations might take.

The activity of mice, cats or other animals

I have already ruled this out as a likely explanation. At most it could only apply to incident (1.) and for reasons already stated does not fit the facts of the case.

Ground water, the vibration of machinery or passing traffic.

As indicated in my first report, close observation revealed that none of these caused any disturbance in either workshop or retail premises.

A Philanthropic neighbour.

In the case of incident 9 it is possible that hearing their requests for Pete to obtain money, a neighbour or customer could have crumpled £5 notes and left them where the witnesses could have found them. This does not explain the notes that appeared at night when the premises were locked, or the coins that arrived in Paul's house.

Lapses of memory in relation to the movement of objects.

It is always possible in the case of displaced objects such as Yvonne's watch, (incident 10), that a witness forgets where something had been left and is then surprised at where in the fullness of time it is discovered. But this could not account for the movement of the stepladders and the other objects, nor could it explain the rubber ball and the child's teddy moved into the ceiling space in incident No. 12.

Tricks in perception.

Particularly in the case of apparitions where the light was poor, it is possible the witness was perceptually deceived. Nevertheless the apparition was reported as presenting the same appearance on each of the three occasions. Furthermore, on the first and second occasions, the sightings were accompanied by projectiles, in one case in the presence of a second witness. If only from a psychological point of view, the variations in Paul's reaction, the second sighting (when one might have expected him to be alarmed by the unexpectedness of the experience but he was not), and to the third (when one might have expected him through familiarity not to be alarmed but he was) also argues somewhat against the idea of perceptual trickery, as does the fact that Paul is thoroughly acquainted with all aspects of the premises. and thus unlikely to be readily deceived by artefacts of light and shadow.

In the context of perceptual error it is also worth noting that, as explained in my first report, the witnesses had no reason to suppose that Pete might in some way be connected with the deceased father of two of them. There had been no suggestion of the involvement of a young boy. This exception '*per se*' seems unlikely to have played a part in Paul's sightings.

Trickery of Persons Unknown

Particularly in the case of incident 7 it is possible that clients or friends visiting the premises could be responsible for jokes at the expense of the witnesses. However such trickery is a much less plausible explanation for the other reported events unless an unidentified third party was in possession of keys to the premises. However I am assured that the only person who had access to keys are the four principal witnesses themselves, and in view of the fact that business people who are improvident enough to lose track of their door keys are unlikely to stay in business for long, I see no good reason to doubt this assurance.

Deliberate fraud by the witnesses

I discussed the possibility of deliberate fraud by the principal witnesses in my first report, and mentioned that all four of them have expressed their willingness to sign sworn statements that they are not responsible for any of the phenomena. I also attested to the reliable nature of the witnesses and to the fact that apparently they have nothing to gain (and potentially something to lose) from the activities of Pete. This initial opinion of the honesty of the witnesses remains unchanged. All four are highly respectable, articulate, and straight-forward people of mature age, whose energy runs into running their business rather that into practical jokes. In the case of incidents where materials or objects have been thrown around and breakages have occurred, the activities of Pete have also involved them in the chore of having to clear up (and indirectly paying for) the damage – a particularly onerous task in the case of the events listed under incident 1.

In any discussion of fraud, it must be recognised that the written word cannot fully convey the reliable and consistent manner in which witnesses give their evidence, or the emotional impact that the experiences recounted in that evidence have clearly had upon them. Thus inevitably a written account depersonalises witnesses somewhat; exposing them in consequence to the scepticism of the critic who has not had direct dealings with them. It also must be recognised that, to the critic, the depersonalisation of the written word may also make those associated with the witnesses appear as gullible people, easily deceived over many months and years even by someone with whom they live or work in close proximity.

Let me assure this critic that all four witnesses in the present case are perceptive and clear headed, know each other intimately, are unlikely in the extreme to be deceived by each other's actions, and never on any occasion have expresses the slightest suspicion of one another. In any context other than the paranormal, their testimony would be accepted without question, and in my view deliberate fraud by any one of them is a virtually untenable suggestion.

Conclusion

Unusual features of the events detailed above are firstly the appearance of the bank notes, and secondly Paul's three sightings of the apparition. To take these in order, the appearance of the money is another example of the "responsive" nature of the poltergeist in the present case. It suggests once more that if the poltergeist phenomenon is genuinely paranormal, it possesses both intent and the rudimentary intelligence necessary to accomplish this event (a suggestion further strengthened by the attempts to lay out cutlery in incident No. 4). There is no obvious way of establishing whether these psychological qualities are in some sense an unconscious projection from the witnesses invalid in the case whether they originate from an independent source. However the coherent nature of the incidents detailed here, and in my first report, inclines me subjectively to favour the latter possibility. The impression - one can put it no more strongly than this – is of a unifying "consciousness" operating in response to, rather than as a result of, that of the witnesses themselves.

In the case of the three sightings of the apparition, it is worth reporting that although sightings of apparitions in connection with poltergeist cases go back at least as far as the celebrated Joller case of 1860-62, they are by no mans common. And cases where synchronicity exists between a sighting and the arrival of a missile are, to my knowledge at least, absent altogether from the literature. In view of the unusualness of this phenomenon, it is relevant to note in the present case that in both instances the missile arrived after the sighting had taken place. Thus there is no possibility that the witness, startled by the missile, imagined he saw something or other at the point from which it apparently originated.

Purely in response to those who claim, 'that once an apparition is reported the power of suggestion may lead others to see it too,' it should be stressed that in spite of their close involvement with all aspects of the phenomena none of the other witnesses report a sighting of any kind. Amongst the witnesses Paul seems in fact to have been the major focus of the activities detailed in this second report on the phenomena and he was also the one most closely involved with the incidents that took place away from the premises. This is consistent with a similar case, where one individual usually seems to supply the physical "energy" upon which the poltergeist is said to draw.

However, absent from this case are both the presence of an adolescent; the suggestion of any strong emotional conflict within or between any of the principal witnesses. One could hardly ask for a more sensible, objective, and well-adjusted group of people. Both they, and I, are at a loss to explain the sudden eruption of these disturbances into their lives, or to account for the strange (though characteristic) attenuation of the "energy," an attenuation which has now led to the virtual cessation of all activity.

But the clear impression is that the phenomena were clearly phenomena of place rather than of person. There is no reliable record of any tragedy occurring on the premises in the recent past, although a customer (I have been unable to trace her) who had read the newspaper article informed two of the witnesses that a small boy was killed in the yard at the back. But nevertheless the "haunting" seems very much to have been associated with the two rooms which go to make up the premises, and the four principal witnesses to have been merely the unwitting human context within which it was allowed physical expression.

Part II of Report written by Professor David Fontana
At the request of the Society for Psychical Research

School of Education, University of Wales, Cardiff

Chapter Ten

THE BOY POLTERGEIST

Professor David Fontana's investigation of the Cardiff poltergeist case, at the request of the Society for Psychical Research (SPR), is what I would describe as a meticulously carried out inquiry. No stone is left unturned, no activity too insignificant to investigate. This is why I have, with his permission, published the second part of his report verbatim.

It has to be said however that time was on his side. His poltergeist was not causing much discomfort to anyone. At times 'he' was actually creating quite a lot of innocent entertainment and mystery for the men cohabiting with him. Throwing stones at an empty shell-case would never be the same for them after 'he' had been removed. Even the carburettor needles stuck in ceilings and walls and human bodies didn't seem to have caused much injury to anyone. Whilst Pete was around there was always a *"funny thing happened at work today"* tale or two to take home to the wife and kids. "The boss just happened to say 'I wish I had something to write with,' and lo and behold a biro pen dropped from the ceiling right by his feet and a minute later a sheet of paper floated down an rested on top of his head. It was this ghost, or whatever, we have in work that did it."

David Fontana's report leaves nothing to chance:

> "However observation over a period or time shows that neither the engineering workshop nor the retail shop are affected by vibration from public vehicles. Nor do they appear to be influenced in any way by the movement of underground water."

I have often felt that when asked to investigate a haunting, members of the SPR always seem anxious to find a natural cause. They give the impression that the last thing they expect or indeed want to find is a ghost.

In his report David Fontana doesn't even tell us that in his opinion the disturbances were caused by paranormal power. He presents the evidence and leaves it to the reader to draw his own conclusion. But I would say, judging by the report, that David himself had to be convinced that the carryings on at this place of work must have been caused by a paranormal activity. As one would expect from the antics being played they were obviously caused by a child spirit. The pranks described in the reports are the typical pranks of a kid. A child always likes a challenge or a dare. For him another person saying, "I wish I had money," or "I wish I had pen and paper," becomes, 'I _dare_ you to find me money," or "I _dare_ you to find me pen and paper." Little Pete also loved to sit a little apart from the men in the yard during their lunchbreaks and to do what little boys love doing best - throwing stones and beating the men at it!

I came across a similar young poltergeist living on his own in a large old house that was being converted into flats. I describe him as a poltergeist because he measures up to my own definition of a poltergeist. I define a poltergeist as a ghost who is able to carry out physical human acts such as throwing a ball or exploding stink bombs!

It was Elwyn Edwards, who later became our researcher, who first told us about this one, and asked our help to get rid of him. He explained to me how, along with others, he had undertaken the task of converting a large house in the village into flats. The work was drawing to a close when trouble struck. The workmen walked out. They believed the house was haunted. There were bangings, they said, strange noises, ice cold rooms, and sounds like a child crying. Somehow the contractor persuaded them to return to work. But a week later they all rushed out again. This time they were all gasping for breath. They swore that someone had released "bloody poison gas" into the house. And this time they were adamant they were not going to return. They also said that the police ought to be called because there was such a dreadful smell in the house they were convinced that there had to be dead body buried in there. Elwyn Edwards told us that what they said about the smell was true. He himself and members of his committee had had the same experience. The awful smell was duly reported to the police and acted upon. Floorboards were lifted, skirting boards taken away, but nothing was found. The house smelt as sweet as one would expect an old neglected house to smell.

Elwyn Edwards and his partners decided to visit Edgar and his wife; the last couple to occupy the house before it was sold for conversion. They traipsed up, a sorry looking crowd of property speculators and investors, to Edgar's front door. When Edgar opened the door to them his first words were: "So you've found the little boy then?" He and his wife then proceeded to tell them more about this little lad.

"Many a night after we had moved into that house," said Edgar, "my wife and I would hear a child crying in the night. And many, many a cold night I would get out of bed thinking it was one of ours. But our three would be fast asleep. Then our children would tell us how, while playing in the garden, they had seen someone with blue, blue eyes watching them through a crack in the hedge." Edgar went on to tell them how one day he had seen the little boy.

"I was digging in the front garden," he said, "I happened to look up and I saw a little boy of about nine or ten standing by the open front door. I remember noticing that he had the bluest of blue eyes I had ever seen. His hair was so blonde that it seemed almost white. I thought he was one of my children's pals and I shouted to him to say the children were all out playing. He stood there for a minute or so and there was a cheeky little grin on his face. He then made as if he was going into the house. I yelled at him to stop, he heard me all right but the little devil was defying me. I put my spade down and sprinted to the house. He was waiting for me at the foot of the stairs. As soon as I arrived at the front door up he scampered, with me after him up the first flight, and when he arrived at the top of the second he turned into the little bedroom and dived under the bed. I could just see his heals sticking out from underneath, I dived and made to get hold of his legs and was just about to say, "*Gotcha!*" when by God it happened. There came a horrible stench from under the bed that made my eyes water and got me gasping for breath. I got out of the house that day quicker than I got in.

"Did you catch him later?" asked Elwyn.

"No," said Edgar, "my sense should have told me not to have made a fool of myself running after him in the first place. I had known for a long time he was hanging around and that it was he who was staring at my children through the fence and crying in his bed at night."

"But who was he?" asked one of the deputation. "Well he is the bloody ghost that's playing tricks with you now isn't he?" said Edgar quite matter of factly. Then he added as an afterthought, "But he's quite harmless y'know. There's no one needs to be afraid of him." But Edwards and his friends knew that once the red ribbon had been cut, the flats declared open and the new tenants had moved in, they would only be safe until Edgar's harmless little boy let out his first whiff of 'spirit gas'. All hell would then be let loose!

It was at this point that Elwyn Edwards came to see me. His plea was genuine: "If you can't get rid of the ghost then for goodness sake get rid of the smell otherwise we will never be able to let the flats."

I knew that Elwyn Roberts, the sensitive, never liked to have pre-knowledge of any spirit activity. It confused him. He much preferred to find the source of trouble for himself. But in this case I decided to brief him about past events. Elwyn decided that it might be a good idea to invite Edgar to join us in our first session. "You see Aelwyn," he said, "if a little boy sees us, a group of strange old men, sitting in a room together inviting him to join us, he would probably run a mile. But he knows Edgar. Probably by now he regards Edgar as a sort of father and there's a chance, with Edgar there, that the little fellow will join us in our circle." Edgar willingly agreed. Elwyn Roberts asked him if he would be willing to undergo light hypnosis for the occasion so that he could see better what was happening. Edgar agreed to this as well ... anything to rid his development of that ghastly smell and the childish pranks of a juvenile ghost.

Our first visitor from the beyond that night was a man in his late 60's who gave his name as Richard Jones. Elwyn told us that he wore a sailor's cap and a navy blue jersey and that he kept wringing his hands and coming in and going out again. He told us that he was a sad looking man and that he kept thinking of him as 'a sailor and yet not a sailor'.

A young woman leading a little boy of about nine by the hand followed him. Elwyn told us that she had come up to him, had pointed to the little boy, and had said, "He was drowned when he was nine years of age. He fell between the boat and a jetty." After that she marched off leaving the little boy with us. The little boy talked to Elwyn. He didn't mention the drowning but he did tell him that he had been on a trip to Llandudno and that he had bought a ball there, and a spinning top. And there was also sufficient information to date the time of his drowning as 1938 or certainly the years before the Second World War.

It reminded me of my own Sunday school trips to Llandudno ten years or so before this little chap's excursions. The first port of call for my parents and me as soon as we got off the train in Llandudno was a large toyshop on Mostyn Street. Here I was allowed to buy a bucket and spade and a beach ball. And then I remembered that I was later allowed to leave the beach, and go with my older brother to a shop in Chapel Street that runs parallel to Mostyn Street. This shop sold the most covetous of merchandise. It had masks and conjuring tricks and it also sold the most potent stink bombs for one halfpenny each. To this day I can still recall the awful stench those stink bombs released. They were like glass marbles and the stinky stuff was the liquid sulphur they contained. When the marbles were dropped on a hard floor the glass would break and the horrible smell would linger until the very last drop of the liquid had evaporated. I think of it now as a period of 15 minutes but it was probably less. It did occur to me that if our little 'polty' lad had visited

Llandudno in 1938 the stink bomb shop would still be there. He told Elwyn that in Llandudno he had bought a ball and a top but he didn't add "and some stink bombs!!" but I have a feeling that at his age, I too would have admitted to buying a bucket and spade but omitted the devil in me that surreptitiously added a couple of halfpenny stink bombs to my shopping list. The follow-on to buying stink bombs was going shares with chums to buy a packet of five Woodbine cigarettes for tuppence.

We had evidence that the ball bought in Llandudno had somehow made it with its owner into the spirit world. It could still to be heard from time to time making bouncing-banging noises as it was thrown against the yard wall of the big house; so why couldn't stink-bombs have made the journey also?

I began to wonder if the 'bloody poison gas' which the workmen complained of had come originally from the shop in Chapel Street, Llandudno.

We found that the little boy's name was Robin Craddock. His mother Elsie Craddock, nee-Jones, had married and Englishman. They lived in Lancashire and the Eccles area was mentioned. But Robin seemed to spend quite a lot of his time in the village of Bala, in North Wales. He also had two best mates in Bala called Alun and Huw and he could also speak a little Welsh. Richard Jones the 'sailor who was not a sailor ' was apparently his uncle.

We tried and tried to find more information about the drowning. He was a Cub Scout and we wrote to every Scout commissioner in the Eccles and south Lancashire area and in Bala to ask if they knew of a Cub Scout having been drowned during this period. Elwyn Edwards searched all manner of records but with little success.

The one thing we all knew for certain was that wherever the little fellow belonged to in his earthly life he didn't belong there any more. We committed his soul to his Creator. Elwyn saw his mother Elsie coming for him one final time. This time he was holding her hand and skipping happily as he went with her to their own place of abode. Edgar also saw the little chap going off with his mother. Edgar under his light hypnosis was sobbing like a child. Large tear blobs running down his cheeks.

When I remembered this incident which happened many years ago, I began to wonder what would have happened to Professor Fontana's 'Pete'. I don't even know if David is a Christian. I'm quite certain that membership of the Christian faith isn't a prerequisite to membership of the SPR for it's probable that many of them are still groping for sufficient evidence that would enable them to believe in a life after death which is a condition of Christian membership. Irrespective the first consideration of a SPR researcher would have been to give a fair assessment of the strange activity in the Cardiff workshop, and the safety of the people passing through this vicinity.

But the clergyman in me has to add that the report ends without showing the slightest concern for the fact that little Pete could be spending the next hundred years throwing stones at an empty shell case, and pinching other people's money to stick on carburettor floats in the home of his favourite humans.

So there we have it.

We have come to the end of the story of two very different entities; Guides and Poltergeists.

Why these two particularly? Jeffrey Archer in his books weaves various plots through the main story which seemingly have no relevance to the reader until you come to the last few chapters then suddenly they become ever so relevant. Guides and Poltergeists while being poles apart share one thing in common and in this 'plot' combine in relevance; they are the only spirit types which are entirely dependent on humans.

Without humans to guard and to protect there would be no role for spirit-guides.

And without humans to leech from there would be no sustenance for poltergeists.

THE EPILOGUE

I have been doing the rounds of haunted houses for more than 50 years. I have tried to help the many families who believed they were being troubled by ghosts; and by doing so, to help the spirits as well.

There have been a few schoolboyish remarks like '*here comes the Ghostbuster!*' at Rural Deanery meetings even though every diocese in Britain has its own equivalent of my appointment.

But when it comes to the push and a ghost does make its appearance on their electoral rolls, my fellow clergy have been very happy to refer the problem to me. Many have been thankful and relieved to have had someone to whom they could pass on the ghostly buck.

With a few of the more evangelical, non-conformist ministers, and those who label themselves 'New Born Christians', things have been rather different. Along the years I have been asked to take part in literally scores of radio and television programmes dealing with the paranormal. Many of these programmes have been of the 'audience participation' kind, or the 'phone-in' type, where – to boost audience ratings - listeners are encouraged to ring the studio with questions and criticisms. The pattern is always the same. The presenter urges me to talk about the ghosts that I have seen and talked to over the years. He does this knowing jolly well that sitting in the audience, or waiting at the other end of a telephone in his home, there will be several irate evangelical gentleman seething at the mouth, itching to lay hands on the microphone to castigate me for my blasphemy. It always breaks out the same way. "How can he, a person who calls himself a "*Man of God*" and a "*Priest of the Church*" say that he has seen a ghost. Doesn't he read the bible! Doesn't he know that to communicate with the dead is a sin!" he'll exclaim. They all then quote reams of verses from one of the early books of the bible, the Book of Deuteronomy. I must admit none of them actually say to me, "You are telling lies," or "You are only saying these things so that you can make money selling your books." Most of them accept that if I say so then I must have both seen something and, where that something is a ghost, spoken to it. But, - and they are all agreed on this - the apparition that I have seen and spoken to was not, they argue, a spirit from beyond the grave. They inform me, quite categorically, that on each and every occasion I have had this experience that I describe as a meeting with a spirit from the beyond, it was, *ipso facto*, a meeting with the Devil himself. They never provide a jot of *ipso*, or an iota of *facto*, to prove their argument. They merely say that whenever such a meeting with a supposed ghost is described it has always been a meeting with the devil. They have belief or knowledge that the devil is able to disguise himself. He can appear as a man or as a woman. To them this is so obvious that it doesn't even call for proof, nor any hint as to the foundation of this information or how their knowledge was obtained or validated. And there is never any exception to this devil rule. It's a form of bigotry. It is never a case of "Sometimes, when I say I have met a ghost, that ghost could have been the devil in disguise." It is not even a ninety nine times out of a hundred chance that he could have been the devil in disguise. They say on every single occasion that I think I have met a ghost, or that anyone else, anywhere in the world, thinks he or she has seen a ghost, it is the devil in disguise that they have seen.

And the programme producer allows them to go on and on with their ranting leaving little time for me refute their arguments. I can only assume that from the media and programme producers point of view, listeners are far more interested in tales of the devil than they are in tales about ghosts; the good-guys.

But I would like to ask these critics and devil-advocates whether they would be prepared to tell Mary Magdalene and the two disciples, Peter and John – all three of them having met Jesus on Easter Day two days after his crucifixion - that it was not the spirit of the crucified Lord that they met at the grave but the Devil disguised as Jesus. And would they be prepared to tell the two sad disciples, on their way home to Emmaus after witnessing the death of Jesus, that the person they met on the road, who had made them so happy, and who had come into their home to break bread with them was not our Lord Jesus, but the Devil disguised as the Son of God.

I have not the slightest doubt that Jesus was a medium. He had, and practised throughout His life, the threefold gifts that all the modern mediums practise.

He had the gift of healing - the Gospels are full of wonderful examples of his daily healing - even my evangelical disputants can't deny this.

He also had the gift of clairvoyance or second sight. There is the lovely tale of His meeting with Nathaniel. When Philip introduced Nathaniel to Jesus, Our Lord said: "Here is a true Israelite in whom there is nothing false." "How do you know me?" Nathaniel asked and Jesus answered, "I saw you whilst you were still under the fig tree before Philip called you."

There is also another lovely example of his clairvoyance and how Christ mischievously uses this gift. This story again is in the Gospel According to St John. Jesus is on His own at a well in Samaria. A Samaritan woman comes to the well to draw water. They talk. Jesus asks the woman if she would like to go and fetch her husband so that he too might hear His teaching. The woman then tells Him: "I have no husband!" Jesus says to her - and one can almost see the roguish look in his eye as he says it – "You are right when you say you have no husband. The fact is you have had five husbands and the man you now have is not your husband. What you have just said is quite true!"

"Sir," the astonished woman says; "I can see you are a prophet." And for prophet, read clairvoyant.

Then in spite of the warning in the Book of Deuteronomy, Jesus also shows that he has the desire and power to speak to spirits of the dead. This story appears in the Gospel According to St Matthew. Jesus takes Peter, James, and John with him to a high mountain. *"There he was transfigured before them, His face shone like the sun, and His clothes became as white as the light. Just then there appeared before them Moses and Elijah talking with Jesus.'*

I have never in my life heard a single clergyman, except possibly myself, referring to this incident as Christ meeting and talking to departed spirits, something that is, according to my disputants, abhorrent to the Lord.

"Let no one be found among you - who is a medium or spiritist or who consults the dead. Everyone who does these things is detestable unto the Lord".

Christian preachers describe this incident as Jesus taking three of His disciples on a little mountain climbing holiday. And surprise, surprise, they almost accidentally meet Moses and Elijah. They must all know that this is not true because Moses and Elijah had been dead for hundreds of years. They could not possibly have met Moses and Elijah. They met, and talked to the spirits, or the ghosts of Moses and Elijah. And furthermore the meeting was no coincidence. This was a planned and premeditated appointment. The crucifixion was looming; Christ, the clairvoyant, could see it clearly ahead. The Jesus who had stripped himself of the godhead was terrified at the thought of it. God was present at this meeting. Jesus received strength. And His disciples were so elated by their experience that they wanted to stay in this place forever. For Peter said; "Lord it is good for us to be here, if you wish I will put up three shelters - one for you, and one for Moses and one for Elijah."

In my book *Yesterday's People* I quote the intellect and research findings of medical doctor Dewi Rees, who in his enquiries into the effects of bereavement, interviewed three hundred women who had been widowed early in their lives. He had asked them if they had seen or felt the presence of their departed husbands. Most of them admitted that they had and described this new nearness as, "A very lovely feeling."

Dr Rees wrote: "The Christian belief in the resurrection is based on the reports of the disciples who met Jesus after His Crucifixion. Similar phenomena are experienced in a lesser way by millions of people today. If the Resurrection of Jesus is true, then the perceptions of the dead by widowed people today must be accorded their own, albeit less significant, reality. It is illogical to accept the one and deny the other, especially as the bereaved report, just like the disciples, that they have heard, spoken to, and been touched by the deceased. This is obviously a difficult issue for the Church to resolve and one can understand the reluctance that Christian leaders may have in approaching it. Nevertheless it is a subject, which needs to be widely discussed. A theology of the Resurrection must remain incomplete if the current experiences of the widowed are not incorporated in it. One cannot say that Christ lives, and that this fact was proven by His reappearance 2000 years ago, but that the perceptions of the dead experienced by many people today have no reality.

We humans are a strange lot. On Palm Sunday, at Easter and at Christmastide we carry armfuls of flowers and lay them on the graves of those we have loved.

But when our loved ones come to our homes to greet us we are scared out of our wits. We call in the ghost-man, and the exorcist, and whoever to shoo them away.

It's a funny old world.

A QUIVER OF GUIDES AND POLTERGEISTS

<u>INDEX</u>

The Author Writes ...

Dear reader,

This is positively my last book on the paranormal and I sincerely hope that you've both enjoyed it and perhaps learned from it.

Publishing is a frustrating and risky business. Not all publishers share my (and *your*) subject interest and when they do, they invariably take fat profits and often demand editorial changes that endanger both the veracity of a book's content and threaten my open and honest way of writing.

Most particularly, they prevaricate. (It's the long lunch-breaks and all the champagne book-launches they attend!). At the age of 84, procrastination in decision-taking is a 'corporate' luxury I can't afford. Some publishers – and I have costly experience of one of them – simply go 'bust'. Spirit Guides are pretty useless in the ways of the commercial world and in advising litigation!

So, in 2001, having experienced megga-publishers handling of umpteen previous books, I set up my own 'publishing house'; **Tegai Publishing**. Immediately the benefits were two-fold. I had control and you – the readers – get a good return on your money. We've cut out a whole chain of middle-men and agents and PR consultants and avoided costly commissions. *"Pob Math"* as they say here in North Wales.

Tegai Publishing (*me!*) – has now bought back is stocks of previously authored books from earlier publishers and at a recent Board Meeting (*me again*), the Marketing Director (*me*) and Financial Director, (*yeah okay, me*) decided to pay out an early dividend to investors (<u>*you*</u>) with addition of many shareholder 'loyalty perks'. The Company Secretary (me) has now written it into the Minutes. For detail, please refer to the facing page.

As the man from Ronson said: *"I liked the product so much ... I bought the company!"*

Aelwyn

Chairman, Chief Executive, Editorial Director, Postroom Boy *et al*
Tegai Publishing – Llandegai, Bangor, North Wales

Tegai Publishing

ORDER FORM

Dear Aelwyn,

I have read "Quiver of Guides and Poltergeists" and now want to
add to my collection of Aelwyn-authored books at discount price.

TITLE	RRP	Discount Price	P&P per copy	No Rqd	☞	TOTAL $0
Holy Ghostbuster	$7.99	$6.00	$1		☞	
Yesterday's People	$7.99	$6.00	$1		☞	
Poble Ddoe	$8.95	$4.25	$1		☞	
Operation Woolsack	$9.95	$5.00	$1		☞	
Privies of Wales	$6.95	$3.99	$1		☞	
Quivers of Guides and Poltergeists	$6.95		$1		☞	

TOTAL | **£** |

Please sign the inside cover, dedicating the book to (name)

_____

And add the short message (approx 10-12 words):

_____

_____

I enclose cheque for | **£** | made payable to: **TEGAI PUBLISHING**

I can expect delivery within 21 days, sent to the following address:

_____

_____

Town

County   Postcode

Your name: (Mr/Mrs/Ms etc)

Return to: Rev. Aelwyn Roberts, Tegai Publishing, Llandegai, Bangor, LL57 4LA, Wales

Aelwyn Roberts …

The Holy Ghostbuster

A ***Quiver of Ghosts and Poltergeists*** is the seventh book published by the Reverend J Aelwyn Roberts, author, television personality, radio broadcaster and retired Anglican clergyman. In his native Wales – where for more than 37 years he was vicar of Llandegai and previously Minor Canon of Bangor's ancient Cathedral – Aelwyn is best known as the *Holy Ghostbuster*, title of his first book chronicling his life's work in dealings with the paranormal.

Aelwyn, a radio broadcaster for more than 50 years, is a popular and often controversial television presenter and commentator; his appearances on ITV, BBCTV, S4C and overseas television varying in subject from Welsh heritage through to the paranormal and more recently into research arguing the true authorship of *"The Works"* of William Shakespeare – basis of his book "*Operation Woolsack*".

He has appeared in the UK in programmes presented by David Frost, Selina Scott and James Whale and has presented his own radio and television series.

Now retired, Aelwyn lives in the quiet village of Llandegai – focal point for his family of six children, 20 grandchildren and one great-grandchild.

For more information, please refer to his website:

www.aelwynroberts.co.uk

Press Reviews ... *of other 'trilogy' books*

THE OBSERVER:
"If there's a ghost on the landing, you just tell it firmly to go away. Theatricals, according to the Rev. Roberts, are not necessary. You don't want to frighten your dead auntie away by waving a crucifix at her!"

SUNDAY PEOPLE:
"*Holy Ghostbuster*" opens an astonishing case-book revealing haunting tales of heartbreak and terror…"

BBCTV:
"The Rev. Roberts has done for communicating with the '*other side*' what Bob Hoskins did for British Telecom … it's good to talk!"

BELLA (Magazine):
"Anglican vicar Aelwyn Roberts says that as a clergyman he had seen many on their deathbeds being met and escorted away by departed relatives…"

DAILY POST:
"A gripping book of ghost stories that is proving to become a best seller…"

DAILY MAIL:
"This book sheds light on the notion that ghosts roam the earth in their millions…"

COUNTY QUEST:
"The most compelling and extraordinary collection of ghost stories I have ever read. This book for young and old should be on every family's Christmas list!"

COSMOPOLITAN (Magazine)
"When you die you got to another more beautiful world. But many can't let go and come back to settle some unresolved business… Rev. Roberts explains all.

CHAT (Magazine)
"Mr Roberts believes there are three main types of ghost … the busybodies, the earthbound and the souls with unresolved earthly problems…."

JOHN WHALE, TV host:
"It's been fascinating …*Wow!*"

CHURCH OF ENGLAND NEWSPAPER
"I like his idea that the past life experiences of regressive patients are simply other spirits using the patient's body…"

PSYCHIC NEWS:
"Challenging traditional Christian teaching on the after-life, Aelwyn Roberts invites us to accompany him on an eye-opening journey into the mysterious world that awaits us.."